7 ESSENTI

Thriving!

~~SURVIVING~~

IN THE WORKPLACE

*To Ricky, my dear,
dear friend and
E. T. with much
love!*

Vicki

Essential Tips for ~~Surviving~~ Thriving in the Workplace
By Vicki Gordon
ISBN: 978-1-312-47286-0
Copyright © 2014 Vicki Gordon

Published in the United States by:
Collins Gordon Group, LLC
402 W Knight Ln
Tempe, AZ 85284

License Notes
All rights reserved. No part of this book may be reproduced in any form or by any means without prior written permission from the publisher except for brief quotations embodied in critical essay, article or review. These articles and/or review must state the correct title and contributing authors of this book by name.

Katherine Norton Collins 1890-1987
Katherine Collins Hicks 1925-2013

For my mother and grandmother whose values and personal examples of perseverance, courage, humor, and unconditional love for me gave me the foundation for a wonderful life.

I also want to acknowledge and thank my husband Bill for his constant, unwavering support throughout almost four decades; Amanda Nicewander for getting me off my duff and convincing me I needed to write this book; and to Ann Wilson, one of my great mentors, a good friend and wonderful editor.

Table of Contents

As I write this message, it has been just a few months since my mother, Katherine, passed away at age eighty-seven, after many years of poor health. She grew up dirt poor in the rural South at the height of the Great Depression, suffered the loss of her father at age thirteen, and endured two bad marriages before finding and marrying my loving stepfather, Raymond. She also gave birth to and reared three children: my brother, John, my sister, Carol Ann—who is profoundly disabled, and whom Mom would always count as one of her life's greatest blessings—and me.

So, though my mother never thought of herself as a strong woman, she *was*, in many, many ways. When my father left us, before my first birthday in 1949, Mom found a job as a bookkeeper in a dress shop in Moultrie, Georgia, making forty dollars a week. Because we couldn't afford a car and there was no public transportation, she walked to work every day.

My equally strong maternal grandmother, Kate, moved in with us to take care of me while Mom worked. So, in the parlance of the time, I was from a "broken home." I can assure you, though, growing up surrounded by the strength and unconditional love of these two amazing women, nothing seemed broken to me!

But Mom wanted me to grow up in the "ideal" family unit that was the norm in the 1950s, so shortly after my seventh birthday she married my first stepfather, sincerely believing he would be a good father to me and a loving husband to her. Sometimes things don't turn out as planned, do they?

My ex-stepfather (henceforth referred to as XSF) was abusive to my mother and me; in fact, it seemed his primary pleasure in life was making us miserable. He took great delight in belittling every accomplishment. We were not permitted to speak at the dining table, and we couldn't have friends over to visit, among a lot of other crazy things. The experience was a huge shock to both of us and a major lesson for me. I discovered that your life can change in an instant.

Another important lesson, though, was that nobody *other* than you can *define* you. I figured out that when life is the most difficult, you just need to keep your wits about you, stay calm, and work your plan—the key point being that you need a plan. Mine was to excel and get out on my own as quickly as I could.

Less than two years after this marriage began, my sweet baby brother, John, was born. My sister, Carol Ann, came along two years later, and we learned right away that "something was wrong." Carol Ann has Down syndrome.

Mom's doctor advised her to let the hospital take Carol Ann and place her in an institution where she could be cared for throughout what would surely be a short life. Mother and XSF were told they could then get on with their lives—whatever that meant.

Mom's response was, "When I leave this hospital, that baby comes with me." Turning over her child to somebody else's care was never an option for Katherine. So Carol Ann came home, and today, fifty-five years later, she lives in a supported apartment, loves life, and brings joy and laughter to everyone who knows her. She's never talked, but she is an excellent communicator!

When XSF finally left I was eighteen, John was ten, and Carol was eight. Mom hadn't worked outside the home in more than ten years, but now she was a single mother again, and she had to find a job. That meant we also had to find care for Carol, which, believe me, wasn't easy back in the 1960s.

I had earned an academic scholarship to Austin Peay State University in Clarksville, Tennessee, and had completed a full year of college. So, Mom and I decided to move the family to Clarksville, a town where there were good job opportunities for the two of us and a school for Carol.

At this point I started to co-parent my sister, participating in all the decisions regarding her care and well-being. Mom and I worked together to get her enrolled in the school, find an after-school caregiver, and do whatever else was needed to keep our lives going.

After completing the second quarter of my sophomore year at Austin Peay, I dropped out to help care for Carol and earn money to support myself. Mom was now working full-time as a bookkeeper, and my brother was in elementary school.

Soon after leaving college I met my first husband, a dashing young lieutenant in the U.S. Army stationed at nearby Fort Campbell, Kentucky. We married after a short courtship, and as soon as he finished his service stint, we moved to his hometown of Minneapolis.

I had always lived in small towns and never outside the South. Moving to a big city in the heart of the Midwest turned my life upside down, and I *loved* it!

Eventually, Mom and Carol even moved to Minneapolis. We enrolled Carol in another school and were able to place her in Mount Olivet Rolling Acres, an incredible facility staffed by loving, caring people dedicated to helping each resident reach his or her full potential.

This was Carol's first time living away from home, and she flourished—so much so that when Mom decided to move back South to marry my stepfather, Raymond, she and I mutually decided I would apply for legal guardianship of Carol so that she could remain in Minnesota with me.

Short courtships are not necessarily always precursors of short marriages, but in my case that sadly was true. At age twenty-four I found myself in a crumbling relationship and knew I had better start thinking of how I was going to support myself long-term.

During my early years in Minneapolis, I had gone back to college and completed two years at the University of Minnesota. But continuing in school didn't seem like an option, as my divorce was being finalized.

So it was at this time I stumbled into the hotel business, a happy circumstance that literally changed my life forever. Interestingly, I was turned down for the first hotel position I applied for, being told I just didn't seem suited for the hospitality business. I'm thinking those years of listening to XSF tell me all the things I *couldn't* do probably strengthened my resolve to prove that hiring manager wrong!

When I landed my first hotel job, in catering sales, I knew right away I'd found my professional niche. It was clear to me I could have a wonderful career in the hotel business, despite my lack of a college degree, if I had a plan and worked my plan. Over the next thirty-six years that proved to be quite true.

Early in my career, I met the wonderful man who would become my husband forever. Bill Gordon was also in the hotel business at that time, but he is a man of many talents. He served twenty years in the U.S. Air Force and then had a twenty-year career in the hospitality industry. He went back to school in his fifties to earn a bachelor's degree, again in his sixties to earn a master's, and once more in his eighties to become an ordained, all-faiths minister. Let me assure you that life with this man has *never* been boring.

Shortly after the dissolution of my first marriage I decided I did not want to have children, so it turned out to be a great blessing to fall in love with and marry someone twenty years older than I was who already had seven grown kids.

Fast-forward to 2008, the year I retired as senior vice president of Corporate Affairs for the Americas region of InterContinental Hotels Group. This was absolutely a dream job for me—I loved everything about it.

My responsibilities included Corporate Communications, Government Affairs, Facilities Management, Meetings and Special Events, and Community Affairs. Having such a diverse and broad range of responsibilities suited me perfectly. I sat on the Americas Management Committee and had an incredible boss who just happened to be president of the region. So, I quit.

Say what? Yes, I decided to retire. I'd worked my plan and achieved success beyond what I could ever have imagined. Bill and I were financially secure, I was at the top of my game, and there were other things to be done. I knew it was time for the next chapter of my life to begin.

Why do I start this business book by telling you all this personal stuff? Because I truly believe the circumstances of our lives shape who we are, but they do not have to define us. My life has been like a lot of other people's lives, filled with ups and downs and ordinary in most ways:

- Father leaves within first year of birth,
- First seven years raised by single mom and grandmother,
- Ten years living with an abusive stepfather,
- Co-parenting a child with severe developmental disabilities,
- College drop-out,
- Divorced by age twenty-five.

Circumstances like these play out day by day, year after year for millions of people. So why do some of these people succeed and others do not? I don't pretend to have the answer to that very complex question, but I do know what worked for me. And that is what I want to share with you in this book. Because you see, that's what the next chapter of *my* life is all about—helping others to help themselves.

If asked what we most want out of life, I'd bet the majority of us would answer, "happiness." Though I haven't conducted a scientific survey, my guess is that it would rank just ahead of "love," or "success."

But when we get the follow-up question, "What would happiness look like for you?" we tend to pause and maybe even stumble and struggle as we try to articulate our own vision of being happy.

Love and success would probably be part of it. We all want to be loved and to be considered good at something, whether it's parenthood or fly-fishing or day-trading or our jobs.

Unless we're independently wealthy, we're going to have to earn a living somehow. For the majority of us, that means we will be in the workplace for a long time—most likely, decades. In fact, for those of us who hold down traditional jobs, our lives will largely be governed by our work. It will determine where we live, our daily schedules, how much vacation, family, and sick leave time we have, and certainly how much money we make.

So, faced with that reality, doesn't it make sense to do everything possible to find fulfillment in the work we do? Of course!

Don't get me wrong. I'm not saying our work or our jobs can make us happy. In fact, a key point of this book is that things outside ourselves—spouses or lovers, friends, money, our work—can't provide happiness. That's our responsibility, and it takes some effort.

Recognizing this, here's some sobering data. In a survey

published in November 2012 by Right Management,[1] the talent and career management expert within ManpowerGroup, 86 percent of employees polled said they planned to actively seek a new position in 2013. Another 8 percent said they might do so and were already networking.

Let's acknowledge that at the time of the survey, the U.S. economy was just beginning to emerge from a deep recession with extraordinary unemployment and under-employment rates. So yes, that could account for a spike in job dissatisfaction levels—but 94 percent of respondents indicating they are actively looking for or considering making a change? That is astonishing.

Chances are that if you're reading this book, you might be part of that 94 percent thinking about making a career change. If so, this book is written to help you make good decisions and take positive action so that wherever you work will be a better place for *you*.

Because we spend so much of our lives at our jobs, the way we choose to relate to our work and workplace has a huge impact on our quality of life, and therefore our level of happiness.

Yes, I did say "choose." That awful company that employs you, the clueless boss, the annoying co-workers, and the mind-numbing work you're asked to do aren't parts of an evil plot that's being perpetrated against you. They are just elements of the circumstances of your life, and each of us has some version of those, in every aspect of our individual worlds.

The choice comes when you have to deal with the circumstances. You can wake up and take responsibility for creating your own happiness at work (and everywhere else). Or you can turn a blind eye to what's really important to you, what you really want, and wake up twenty or thirty years later still doing a job you hate, or that at best you find boring. As John Lennon famously said, "Life is what happens to you while you're busy making other plans."

Here's how the process works: Creating happiness starts with going to the trouble of defining your values, goals, and ambitions. Only by investing the time to do your personal homework and truly understanding yourself can you have a chance of knowing happiness when you experience it.

The second part of the equation: Live your life (especially at work) being true to yourself—honoring your values, pursuing your goals, and striving to realize your ambitions.

That's it. No, really—it *is* that simple, and that difficult. How do I know? Because I've proved it to myself again and again throughout my career. Let me tell you a story about that.

Around fifteen years ago I was in a good place in my work life. I was a vice president for a major hotel company, and for years I had received nothing but glowing performance reviews and steady advancement. At this particular juncture, I was given an exciting, challenging assignment. Sounds like a dream come true? Wait for it . . .

Not long into the project, the company underwent yet another reorganization, and I got a new boss. He didn't like me, and I certainly didn't like him. He was a real jerk who took every opportunity to let me know that I wasn't a "good fit" with his team.

I dreaded staff meetings, and I practically

hyperventilated when I had to have a one-on-one conversation with this man. I just knew he was looking for a reason to fire me.

For months I wallowed in self-pity and inertia. Finally, I reached the breaking point. I called in sick and took a mental health day. And on that day, I faced my situation and understood that inertia was death by a thousand cuts. I realized I had to let go of my anger and righteous indignation and make a plan.

Right then and there I made up my mind that if nothing had improved within thirty days, I'd resign. And I resolved to use the coming month to prepare myself for the worst-case scenario.

I was still stressed, but I immediately felt better because at least I was being proactive. Realizing that if I was going to be job-hunting I would need to look my best, I decided to get my health and fitness act together. I'm a stress eater, and in the months since I began working for the new boss, I had packed on the pounds. So I joined Weight Watchers® and began to drop the excess baggage (eventually I lost eighty pounds during the course of eighteen months).

It also occurred to me that I needed to develop a network of acquaintances outside my current co-workers (*hello!*). While I was losing the weight, I started checking out volunteer opportunities and professional associations where I could meet and mingle with like-minded people. This arena ultimately became a huge priority for me, and one that has made my life significantly richer.

Step Three in the plan was to find out what my options were, should I indeed be terminated. While investigating severance packages for my position's grade level, I also made discreet inquiries about other internal job opportunities.

It felt good to take some action. I had a sense of being more in control of my fate, despite the fact that not all the answers I found were what I wanted them to be. But I was now better informed and could make more realistic plans.

A funny thing happened as I went through this process. I stopped being scared and depressed and started actually being excited about my prospects, both within and outside the company.

Here's how the story ends: In the course of my reconnaissance on my own company—the company where, at that point, I had worked for almost ten years—I discovered a gap that I was perfect to fill. An executive I knew slightly had recently been promoted into a job that placed him in somewhat unfamiliar territory. He needed someone to help him communicate with an entirely new internal audience, but he didn't fully realize it yet. So I approached him with a proposal for a new role for myself doing just that, and he went for it.

He created a position for me, reporting directly to him, and set it up so that every piece of communication going to the field went through me, across all departments within the organization. I worked for him for several years, including when he was transferred to Europe to become vice chairman of the company.

Shortly after I took on this new assignment, the boss I had not enjoyed working with left the company to work for a competitor.

As for me...well, I got excited about my company, and my career, all over again. There was also an interesting by-product. You guessed it—happiness, and not just in my job, but in my relationships with my husband, family, and friends, as well as my outlook on life.

Did the "happy times" last? Yes, for several years. But when the next challenge arose at work, I was ready for it. I had a plan and an approach with a proven track record, and they served me just as well in that situation, and the next, and the next.

That's why I decided to write this book—to share with you what I've discovered about the ability each of us has to deal powerfully and effectively with our circumstances. In particular, I want to show you how to shift your relationships with your job from "hating" or "tolerating" what you do to earn a living to really being excited and energized by coming in to work every day.

And I have good news for you. You already know how to do this. You've got the secret code—it just may be encrypted. This book will show you how to break that code.

Let's start with a closer look at your relationship to your job. Take a moment and answer these questions as honestly as you can: Do you love what you do every day for a living? No, I mean do you really, *really* enjoy your work?

Here's another statistic to chew on: A number of recent studies indicate that a surprisingly small percentage of the population of the United States—as little as one-fifth, according to some reports—are "satisfied" with their jobs. And that's just being satisfied, not necessarily feeling wildly excited about their work. That leaves a pretty significant majority who don't like their jobs and/or wish they could leave (which takes us back to the 94 percent who are looking to make a change).

What's wrong here? Sure, there are lots of reasons to be discontented. You may be feeling the pressure of having to do the same or more work with shrinking resources, if your company is one of those that have cut staff and budgets or steadfastly refused to hire new employees to fill positions that come open.

Or, you may feel trapped in a job that isn't bad, but doesn't exactly light your fire or offer much in the way of a career path.

You may be feeling vulnerable because you're the newest hire or the one who's been around the longest and is only a few years away from retirement.

Regardless of the category you may be in, if you didn't answer the two questions above with a resounding "Yes!" then this book is for you. And even if you did, the process and action steps defined in each chapter will help you up your game and find higher levels of satisfaction and success.

Your workplace doesn't have to be your prison. It doesn't even have to be some sort of purgatory, a way-station where you toil joylessly for years and years until you can finally retire—if you can ever retire. What a dim prospect for how to spend your twenties, thirties, forties, fifties, and maybe even beyond!

But chances are you picked up this book because that's how you feel about your job and what you believe you are facing in your career. You're stuck, and aren't sure how to get unstuck. I know a little something about that.

I'm going to tell you another story. In fact, you'll find this book is filled with stories—a few from my life, but more from people in a variety of jobs and industries who have crafted successful careers for themselves, sometimes in unusual ways and despite less-than-positive circumstances. I think you'll find their workplace experiences and insights just as enlightening as I did.

But back to my story about being stuck. When I was a kid in South Georgia in the 1950s, most of the homes in our neighborhood had big front porches so you could sit outside and catch a breeze, out of the glare of the hot sun. One day when I was about five years old, I was at Dottie Thomas's house, and we were playing on her front porch. Somehow—to this day, I have no idea how—I got my head caught between the spindles on the porch railing. I couldn't get it out!

Dottie ran inside to fetch her mother, who hollered down the street to my grandmother. (Grandma looked after me while my mother was at work.) While the two ladies were desperately trying to figure out how to get me unstuck without injuring me or tearing down the porch, I was wriggling, crying, and carrying on as only a five-year-old can do. In short, I was pitching a bona fide hissy fit.

Finally, Grandma said to me in no uncertain terms, "Vicki, be still!" I always minded my Grandma, so I just got still. And once I got still, I got unstuck.

You see where I'm headed with this story, right? We all get stuck at some point in our work lives. We find ourselves in a situation that just seems impossible, or hopeless, or both. And we start to flail around, worrying desperately about the future, wondering what we did wrong in the past, blaming the company, blaming our bosses, our co-workers, the economy (or all three), and usually blaming ourselves, too. And the more we flail around, the more stuck we get.

The number one goal of this book is to help you "get

still," so that you can get unstuck. It's designed to support you in first quieting down the "chatter" in your head—all the blaming, judging, and worrying—so that you can actually hear and feel what speaks to your heart and that you love to do. Then, it provides a step-by-step guide for recreating your career as you want it to go.

You may discover that your path to fulfillment in the workplace leads to a different organization or industry. Or, you might see that staying right where you are, but shifting your relationship to your company and job, opens up a whole new realm of opportunity—for enjoying the work you do now, for learning about positions in other departments that interest you, or for sourcing projects, events, and initiatives in which you may want to become involved.

But the overall result will be getting in action—not just doing things and being busy, but making well-thought-out moves that advance you toward a specific objective you have chosen that holds meaning for you.

And while the guidelines in this book are written with corporate employees in mind, they work just as well for anyone who has a role to play in any organization. Whether you're an entrepreneur getting a new business off the ground, a busy mom trying to manage her family, or a volunteer for a local charity, this book can help you.

Your journey starts with a reintroduction to someone you've probably not taken the time to catch up with in a while—yourself. In Chapter One, you'll do some self-examination about what your own personal definition of success looks like. That will involve understanding what's truly important to you, getting clear about what you really do and don't want to do in your career and life, and coming to terms with the importance of leadership and power in realizing your dreams and goals. You'll also get some good advice about staying focused once you've determined your success parameters.

Then, with a solid, inspirational vision of what you want in hand, you'll start exploring how to get it. Chapters Two, Three, and Four walk you through the all-important basics of assessing the lay of the land—the critical "homework" you need to do to understand your work environment and the key players.

How well do you know the company you work for? In Chapter Two, you'll self-test your knowledge about your employer's business model, and do some thinking about why the more you know about what makes your company tick, the better your chances of finding the perfect niche where you can make a contribution and shine.

Just as important as knowing your company is understanding the person you work for. Chapter Three helps you see your working world through the eyes of your boss. By putting yourself in his or her shoes, you'll be better able to make subtle changes in how you approach requests, reports, and day-to-day communication that will have a tremendous positive effect on this important relationship.

The third leg of the stool in creating a sound basis for reenergizing your career and work life is to develop a keen appreciation for what the folks in Human Resources may—and may not—be able to do for you. Chapter Four is designed to open your eyes to the role this pivotal function plays in virtually every organization, and how you can use the HR department's information, skills, and services to maximum advantage.

So you've done your due diligence and built the foundation—now what? Chapters Five and Six prompt you to move beyond your comfort zone and take your career inquiry deeper and wider. Do you have a mentor or mentors? Have you ever thought about seeking one out? You'll examine the pros and cons of being mentored in Chapter Five and get some tips for making the most of the wisdom, connections, and perspective that a mentor can provide. This chapter also introduces some best practices you can take on to expand the breadth and richness of your thinking, starting by actively seeking out viewpoints on ideas and issues that are different from your own.

At this point in your exploratory journey, you'll likely have begun to see where you can really bring value and make a difference, and Chapter Six will help you home in on those areas of opportunity. You'll see how to take the game up a level, by looking not just at the different existing places within (or outside) your company where you might be a perfect fit, but by examining where and how you could create new career opportunities where none existed before.

By Chapter Seven, you'll be in the homestretch. You'll have your eyes on the prize, and the priority and challenge will be to stay focused on getting all the way "there"—into a new position, taking on additional or different responsibilities, or simply reframing how you relate to the job you have.

Now you'll be able to take a deep breath and congratulate yourself on transforming your life at work! Chapter Seven encourages you to take some time to reflect on the bigger picture—to consider the lasting impact you want to have on the people and organizations you interact with, and the difference you may want to make for the world. Yes, *you!*

Are you ready to get started? Just a couple of suggestions before we launch.

First, I recommend that you read through each chapter, then go back and actually *do* the exercises they contain. Reading over the questions and forms is a good start, but you won't get maximum value from this book unless you take the time to complete the work laid out chapter by chapter. You may even want to get a small notebook where you can keep your responses to the exercises, along with the observations, insights, and learning you glean as you go through this process.

Finally, relax, and open your mind. This book will ask you to view your workaday world in a completely different way than you have before. Leave your preconceived notions and old ways of thinking outside the door, and anytime you sense them intruding, kick them out!

Invest some time and effort now and reap the rewards for the longer term. Get ready to thrive in the workplace!

1. Right Management surveyed 760 employees in the United States and Canada via an online poll that ran from October 15 to November 15, 2012.

CHAPTER ONE

DEFINE YOUR OWN SUCCESS
... and focus like a long-distance runner

To laugh often and love much; to win the respect of intelligent persons and the affection of children; to earn the approbation of honest citizens and endure the betrayal of false friends; to appreciate beauty; to find the best in others; to give of oneself; to leave the world a bit better, whether by a healthy child, a garden patch, or a redeemed social condition; to have played and laughed with enthusiasm and sung with exultation; to know even one life has breathed easier because you have lived—this is to have succeeded.
—Bessie Anderson Stanley (often incorrectly attributed to Ralph Waldo Emerson)

Wherever you are in your career trajectory, you can't be successful in the fullest sense unless you know where you want to go. That means defining, accepting responsibility for, and being consciously willing to make the trade-offs required to achieve that success.

Shakespeare had Hamlet advise, "To thine own self be true." But how can we be true to ourselves if we don't *know* ourselves? When we allow someone else (a boss, a spouse, a parent) to define who we are, we lose our ability to discover, grow, and develop.

We've all heard many times that you can't know which path to take unless you are clear about where you're going. Likewise, not knowing where you want to go leads to indecisiveness, insecurity, and frequently, bad temper. *Yikes!*

What does this mean for your life and career aspirations? Think about it: Would you want to follow a leader who is insecure, indecisive, and in a bad mood? Didn't think so. Well, neither does anyone else.

This takes us back to the importance of defining and owning your success. For many, the definition of success involves leadership in some form. It may mean being a leader in your family, in your community, in your place of worship, or in the workplace. Since this book is all about thriving in the workplace, we'll focus on leadership as it pertains to your career.

You can't be the kind of leader people want to follow unless you can clearly articulate your vision and how you intend to get there. This is especially true in the workplace, so remember this as you consider how others view you.

For me, defining my own success took a while. By that I mean I was in my forties and well into my career before I got it right. So don't despair if you're a couple of decades in and are still struggling to figure out your path. The advice offered in this book is designed to help accelerate your journey regardless of where you're beginning.

Of course, investing the time to understand what you truly value and want in your career is a beneficial exercise at any point. The earlier you make the investment, the bigger the dividends. I like to draw the analogy of compounding financial investments. Albert Einstein called compound interest "the greatest mathematical discovery of all time." Indeed, the principle of compounding can be applied to everyday life.

Through the magic of compounding, an early investment in self-assessment can be transformed into a powerful, happiness-generating tool over the course of a lifetime. Compounding, in my terms, is the process of generating dividends on an individual's reinvested knowledge of self.

This personal compounding requires two things to work: the reinvestment of an ever-increasing understanding of one's goals, and time. The more time you give this process, the better you are able to accelerate the payoff on your original investment.

Fortunately I've had good instincts all along, which led to some early decisions that ultimately served me well. But it was a journey, I can assure you.

Defining my own success meant taking a long, honest look at what was truly important to me—and what wasn't. It meant not accepting someone else's definition of success, no matter how well-intentioned that person (or persons) might be.

The process involved a lot of introspection and the willingness to move beyond simple answers. Finally, over a number of years I came to realize that success, for me, wouldn't be measured by title, income, or the other typical trappings. For me, it was about power.

Now, hold on! I'm not talking about the type of power personified by Gordon Gekko in the "Wall Street" movies. I mean the power to make a difference, whether by influencing policy and behaviors in the workplace or through personal philanthropy and volunteerism.

When I first started in the hospitality industry, my idea of success was to be the owner of a large, profitable hotel. One of the steps along the way toward that version of success was to own a restaurant. I found out very quickly that I'm not, by nature or inclination, an entrepreneur. Good to know.

Based on that invaluable learning experience, I redefined my measure of success as becoming general manager of a large, successful hotel. This time I discovered I really didn't like operations. Also good to know, and a much less expensive lesson than owning a restaurant, I can assure you.

After much soul-searching it became clear to me that I loved working in a corporate environment and on the creative side of the business. From that moment on I was moving! Throughout the next ten years, my career quickly gained speed as I rose from Director of Product Marketing to Senior Vice President of Corporate Affairs for the Americas Region of InterContinental Hotels Group (IHG), one of the world's largest hotel companies.

For the last nine years of my corporate life, until I retired from IHG in 2008, it was my great pleasure to serve as a senior policy advisor for the company in areas that ranged from communications, crisis response, and business continuity planning to government affairs, corporate travel, and community relations. This role was absolutely my sweet spot, and I thoroughly enjoyed every minute of it!

So why leave such a wonderful career? Because an important part of success is knowing when it's time to celebrate goals achieved and go on to the next great thing. I love this quote by seventeenth century Spanish Jesuit Baltasar Gracian: "Quit while you're ahead. All the best gamblers do." Seventeenth century Spanish Jesuit—go figure...

I was ready to move beyond success to significance, to build on all the things I'd done and accomplished—both professionally and personally—to truly make a difference in the world.

Let me give you an example of someone whose career path wasn't quite as linear as mine. Jacqueline (Jacqui) Welch is a smart, strong businesswoman who has worked her way up to the senior ranks of Human Resources professionals. Her path, though, was pretty circuitous—on the surface.

As an undergrad, Jacqui was a pre-med major. During a summer as an intern for a big pharmaceutical company, she saw first-hand that medicine in the United States is a big, for-profit business. With her altruistic vision brought into real-world focus, she realized this wasn't the path for her.

She switched her major and got a degree in English. In her junior year, she worked in Human Resources for the Urban League of Onondaga County, in upstate New York. An experience there changed her life dramatically.

In Jacqui's words, "I placed someone in a position—a big, powerful-looking man—and he actually cried for joy at getting the job. At that moment something clicked for me, and I knew I'd found my path."

From this point, Jacqui began to think more strategically about her career goals and aspirations. She took a job in retail to get into a management training program that offered tuition reimbursement, and used it for graduate school. With a master's degree in human resources in hand, she moved forward along her career journey, striving to build broad strategic skills that would keep her from being pigeonholed in one particular niche.

Jacqui says her mantra has always been, "Have a plan, but be flexible." As fate would have it, she reconnected with an old friend who worked for Towers Perrin (now Towers Watson), a consulting firm specializing in human resources and financial services. One conversation led to another, and Jacqui ended up joining Towers Perrin because the firm had the clients, engagements, breadth of work, and travel opportunities she knew would help hone her skills.

After two years of critically valuable experience with this company, Jacqui was recruited by consulting giant Accenture. During her five years there she worked in the firm's technology practice, deepening her skills and expertise in an area that was growing by leaps and bounds.

Up, up, up the ladder, she was flying somewhere almost every week. In her seventh year of consulting, she—as every American— was stunned by the events of September 11, 2001. She couldn't help thinking it might have been her on one of those planes.

She had come to understand that consulting was not only a career but a lifestyle. And she realized after 9/11 it wasn't a lifestyle she wanted. So, in her partner-making year at Accenture, Jacqui decided to leave. Why? Because she understood herself well enough to know that the financial rewards and fast-paced lifestyle of a consultant did not constitute her personal definition of success. "For me, family is my number one priority," she says. "I only have one shot to be my husband's wife and my children's parent."

So did she step off the career path? Far from it. Jacqui went on to spend five very productive years in Human

Resources for RockTenn, now a ten-billion-dollar paper and packaging company, and from there moved even higher up the ladder to become senior vice president of Global Talent Management for Turner Broadcasting, parent company of CNN.

Remember my earlier remark about Jacqui's career seeming at first glance to be pretty circuitous? Let's look at that. She shifted from pre-med to English major, and from positions in retail and HR consulting to corporate HR roles with a paper and packaging manufacturing company and then one of the world's leading broadcasting organizations. Initially, these seem like very different jobs. What they have in common is that Jacqui used every one of them to acquire new skills and expertise that eventually positioned her to step into a senior HR leadership role. She has now done that quite successfully.

Along the way, Jacqui discovered that her definition of success involved more than having a high-powered career. It also meant focusing on her family and taking on professional roles that enabled her to do that. She is a woman who knows what she wants and where she's going.

Understanding yourself and getting clear about what's important is, of course, a personal and completely individual process that looks different for each of us. Here's another thought-provoking success story of a different kind.

This was told to me by Gale Buckner, a longtime friend and role model. Gale has worked in the justice system for many years, with the Georgia Bureau of Investigation, as director of the Department of Juvenile Justice for the State of Georgia, on the Board of Pardons and Parole (eventually serving as chair for two years), and in her current role as chief magistrate of Magistrate Court in Murray County, Georgia.

When Gale shared this account with me over breakfast recently, it made my spirits soar and reinforced my belief that bad things don't have to derail us or our dreams. The story began with a seven-year-old boy seeing his mother dragged from their home and beaten to death in the driveway by his father, the mother's ex-husband. Surely not one of us could ever imagine a more terrifying and traumatic experience.

The child was put into the foster care system and drifted into truancy, substance abuse, and other bad behaviors. Gale interacted with this young man in the juvenile justice system, where she has seen many young lives destroyed by tragic family circumstances and poor life choices.

But this story has an ending you might not have predicted. Gale told me that, because of a number of successful interventions, the young man now lives in Florida and is a successful entrepreneur with his own lawn care business. He mows lawns.

Without knowing any of the history, this might not seem like a major accomplishment. But this young man's definition of success consisted of staying clean and sober, keeping out of trouble with the law, supporting himself, and feeling good about himself. On his own terms, he has indeed achieved success!

By this time you may be thinking, "All right, I'm ready to define my own success. But how do I *do* that?" The questionnaire below is designed to get your thought process started. Take the time to truly consider all the questions and be rigorously honest in your answers. They will no doubt trigger other questions. This is a good thing!

Diagnostic Questionnaire for Defining My Success

Is my job part of who I am, or is it a means to an end?

_____

Am I doing what I want to do or what I'm educated/trained to do? Or both?

_____

Do my skills support my chosen career path? [2]

_____

What do I like to do for fun? Is this something I dream of doing for a living?

_____

Would I be doing the work I'm currently doing if I didn't get paid for it?

_____

Where and how do family and career intersect for me? What are my priorities and boundaries?

_____

Rank the following in order of importance to you, listing most important first:
1. Building personal wealth
2. Time for interests/activities outside work
3. Family time
4. Being active in the community
5. Being recognized as successful
6. Being a leader

7. Fame

When you've completed this assessment, you should have a much clearer picture of what *you* want out of life. Maybe it's the corner office, a leadership role in business and all the perks that come along with that. Or maybe for you it means being able to leave work at the end of an eight-hour day and volunteer in the community or spend time with your family and friends.

While defining success for yourself is the first, critically important step toward thriving in the workplace, there's an equally important accompanying practice I recommend that you take on: Focus like a long-distance runner. This involves much more than committing to "never give up" and "follow your dreams." It includes those things, but it's also about recognizing destructive emotions and behaviors that are so subtle and subversive, we often don't know they are shaping our lives. The emotions I'm talking about are jealousy, envy, and insecurity. These insidious feelings can taint our view of the work environment and co-workers, often overpowering even the most talented and best-intentioned of us.

Let me illustrate this point with an unpleasant scenario in my life that kept repeating until I forced myself to do an honest assessment and come face-to-face with my own self-destructive behavior.

On more than one occasion I was promoted and moved into jobs I could never have imagined for myself—positions that helped propel me up the career ladder at a pretty impressive pace, and I relished every new challenge. Each successive role brought opportunities to learn new skills and flex my creative muscle. I had the chance to travel to parts of the world I'd never seen and interact with interesting people. Repeatedly I would think how "lucky" I was to have these incredible, exciting experiences.

Then my insecurities would start to do their thing. In my case, feeling "lucky" undermined my sense of achievement at having *earned* these roles through smarts, a strong work ethic, and demonstrating my value to the organization.

The insecurities led to envy and jealousy. I'd look around at my peers and think, "I know she makes more money than I do. I'll bet she's a higher grade level than I am, too, and that's not fair. I'm just as smart, my job is just as important, blah, blah, blah—

Does this sound familiar? If so, let me give you some advice. Get over yourself! You need to focus like a long-distance runner. This means not being distracted by the other runners. It means keeping your eyes directed straight ahead on your own goals and objectives. Your chances of crossing your own self-defined finish line for success go up exponentially when you keep your attention on what *you* are doing, not what somebody else is doing.

Finally, do you enjoy doing the work you do? Are you on your chosen path? If the answers to those two simple questions are yes, then focus on how you can keep improving yourself. Don't lose your way to success because you're too busy worrying about the other guy. Trust me, that is *not* going to make you happy.

And if the answers to the two questions were no, or if you feel your life is out of balance, then try this simple exercise that Jacqui Welch came across in a time management class. Account for every minute of a twenty-four-hour period of your life, jotting down things like commute time, sleeping, and so on. Then look at your list of activities and ask, "What have I created for myself? What can I let go of?"

Let me tell you, this little exercise is a real eye-opener. When I took it and realized how much time I was taking every day just for "idle chitchat," I was stunned. My first reaction was, "I gotta cut that out!" Upon further consideration, though, I realized that chitchat is my way of connecting with friends, learning new things, and experiencing the joy of human interaction. All of that is very important to me, so I came to accept the fact that, for me, chitchat isn't a time-waster, it's a joy-giver.

Okay, it's your turn to take the exercise. Looking at all the minutes you use in the course of a day doing things that don't bring you joy may not be necessary, and are sometimes just mindless. Do you need to make some adjustments? Most of us do, and we have to do so fearlessly. Remember something else Jacqui says about this exercise: "Most people love your boundaries as long as they are inside them . . ."

Now, take a moment to go back to the beginning of this chapter and reread the quote from Bessie Stanley. Notice that nowhere in that description of success is there any mention of material wealth or social position. The quote reflects Stanley's personal definition of success (that I share, by the way), but it may or may not be yours.

Once you've settled on *your* definition of success, create your own quote. Write it here, but keep it in your heart.

2. *Harvard Business School senior associate dean and management professor Robert Kaplan advises, "Take ownership of understanding your skills."*

CHAPTER TWO

UNDERSTAND THE ORGANIZATION
...to find your unique niche.

I have long been profoundly convinced that in the very nature of things, employers and employees are partners, not enemies; that their interests are common, not opposed; that in the long run the success of each is dependent upon the success of the other.
—John D. Rockefeller, Jr.

-

All good leaders know the importance of having the entire organization aligned behind a shared vision and mission. *Great* leaders also realize that knowledge is power and that they can empower their employees by ensuring everyone working in the organization—whether nonprofit, for-profit, or public sector—are clear about not only its mission but also its business model. **3**

Why is it so important to understand how an organization sustains itself and prospers? One obvious answer is that if the organization can't sustain itself it implodes, and people lose jobs. Those receiving the goods and services of the organization lose their supply source. Not good.

Every business entity, including nonprofits and public sector companies, must have income in order to do business. It's more widely understood that the private sector works to produce profits, but *all* organizations must generate revenue in order to function, through sales, government appropriations, grants and donations, taxes and fees, or some other source.

Leaders of organizations are expected to know every possible revenue source and how to maximize those revenues. They in turn should expect everyone else in the enterprise at minimum to understand the business model. If employees don't have this basic grasp of the organization's operations, how can they be effective in helping it succeed?

Let me share an example from my thirty-six-plus years in the hotel industry. Early on I worked in individual hotels where the revenues were almost entirely from guest room and food and beverage sales.

Over the years, as technology flourished, hotels began to reap additional revenues from more unlikely sources: in-room telephone charges, Internet connections, and on-demand, interactive television offerings such as games and movies.

Throughout the past decade and a half we've seen technological advances leapfrog themselves on what seems like a daily basis, and a number of these have impacted previously lucrative hotel revenue centers. Cell phones have become ubiquitous, making in-room telephone charges virtually obsolete. The same thing happened with revenues from Internet connection charges, as high-speed Wi-Fi has become an expected complimentary amenity in most hotels.

This is a telling demonstration of how, in a relatively short period of time, revenue streams can change even in a business environment that outwardly appears relatively unchanged. Hotels still offer essentially the same core product they always have—lodging, food, and beverage.

As my career progressed I became part of the management team of a large hotel company that franchises most of its hotels. I learned that the business model was very different in that environment. Franchisees pay the franchisor royalty fees, licensing and relicensing fees, application fees, marketing fees, technology fees, and income related to loyalty programs, among a number of other obligations. From the outside it's still the hotel business, but inside resides a much more complicated business model.

For you, as an employee seeking to add value or find new opportunities aligned with your own definition of success, it's important to know where to look. Makes sense, doesn't it? Fish where the fish are.

Using the example above, three important things stand out regarding why it's important to know how an organization generates revenue. The first is that being aware of all the various revenue sources increases the likelihood that you will identify an opportunity to make a contribution adding value.

Here's how that might work: Let's say your employer organization has a large customer loyalty program. You have a job in the Finance Department, not the Loyalty business unit, but you take the initiative to learn about the different ways the loyalty program brings in money for the company. This could be through things like affinity credit cards and direct marketing fees to advertisers, in addition to ongoing business from loyal customers.

Using your finance background you identify a significant, untapped revenue maximization opportunity. With the backing of your supervisor and the head of Finance, you take this concept forward to senior management, provide substantiation for your theory, and ask for the challenge of leading the implementation of your idea.

You've just added value for the organization. And along the way, your star has gained a little luster. Not a bad outcome for devoting the time to take apart the "clock" and learn how it works, right?

Here's the second good reason to be sure you know how your organization ticks: it will give you a much greater understanding of internal priorities. For instance, if your company has only $100,000 to spend on technology improvements in a given year, how does that funding get allocated?

If you don't completely understand *how* the business where you work makes money, it's probably going to be tough to accept *why* a project near and dear to your and/or your department's heart keeps getting cut from the priority technology projects list. We've all heard, and yes, most likely participated in, the sad refrain, "Doesn't anyone besides me understand how important this is?"

Take a minute for the following simple exercise about establishing technology upgrade priorities for a theoretical company. Look over the list below and assign a priority ranking to each item. Use a scale of one to five, with one being the highest priority.

- Increase credit card security for website transactions
- Upgrade company intranet to offer online benefits enrollment.
- Implement an employee volunteer time tracking system.
- Create an employee identification system based on bio-metric information such as retinal scan, fingerprinting, and so on.

- Upgrade the customer loyalty program to provide online tracking of purchases and spending history/patterns.

You're probably thinking, "How in the world can I assign priorities when I don't even know what the business is and how it works?" Well, that's the point, isn't it?

Now look at the same list and designate priorities for each of the following entities, based on their organizational profiles:

- A global, business-to-consumer (B2C) enterprise selling patented, cutting-edge products, primarily via the Internet
- A nonprofit organization heavily dependent on volunteers for delivery of goods and services
- A service industry company whose labor force is the primary operating expense

That was a good bit easier, wasn't it? And you see where I'm going with this. No organization has unlimited financial resources, so prioritizing spending is *always* necessary. While it still may be tough to come to terms with the fact that your funding request has been denied, it's a heck of a lot easier to get over it if you're aware of the priority rationale.

This may sound simplistic, but experience has shown me that a generally held, basic understanding of the business leads to a more harmonious workplace and makes it easier for employees to rally behind a shared vision and mission.

Too often resentments build between individuals and departments because one is seen as "favored" though the other works just as hard, does as good a job, and so on. When pretty much everyone embraces prioritizing as a fact of life—business or personal—each person is then empowered to make more informed individual choices. You can love what you do but accept where your work or project falls on the organization's priority charts. Or, you can position yourself to move on to something that's a better fit with your goals and aspirations.

Finally, a more in-depth, robust understanding of how your organization works provides a platform for personal growth and advancement. How often have we heard stories of leaders who started with a company in an hourly position, often as a summer job, only to rise through the ranks to become president or CEO?

It happens, but never by chance. Only you can cause success scenarios—however you define them—to become a reality. So let's pause here for you to assess your knowledge of your own organization.

How Does Your Organization Generate Revenues?

Which of these describes how your company sells its goods and/or services?
___ Business-to-Business (B2B) Sales
___ Business-to-Consumer (B2C) Sales

What are the company's specific sources of revenue? Check all that apply:
___ Taxes and Fees
___ Grants
___ Services
___ Manufacturing

___ Licensing/Royalties
___ Other

What are the various revenue centers within your organization? Again, check all that apply:
___ Direct Sales
___ Licensing Fees
___ Service Contracts
___ "Bricks & Clicks" (retail presence—stores—and/or online sales)
___ Product Add-Ons
___ Other

Now, the moment of reckoning has come. What if you don't know the answers to these basic questions about your company? How do you find out? Whom do you ask?

Though this differs across organizations, a good place to start is often with your supervisor. Kirk Kinsell, president of the Americas region for InterContinental Hotels Group (IHG), says, "Just ask. Start with your boss, and if you don't get the information you're looking for, talk with someone in senior management or Finance."

Doing so will certainly demonstrate you are an employee who wants to do more than just "put in your time." By showing this level of interest, you're demonstrating a desire to add value to the organization.

If you work for a publicly held company, the information it must, by law, make available is another good resource. This material, such as the annual report and SEC filings, is usually posted on the corporate website.

Nonprofit organizations also must make certain information public and usually include it on their websites. You can learn a lot just by taking the time to read something as seemingly mundane as an annual report.

Most larger public companies also hold "quarterly earnings calls" for market analysts and investors. An earnings call is a <u>teleconference</u>, or increasingly a webcast, in which a <u>public company</u> discusses the financial results of a reporting period via an 800 number and on the Internet. These are another rich source of useful information about a company. Call schedules, how to access calls and often recordings of past calls are quite often available on the company website. According to Jacqui Welch, the Human Resources executive you met in Chapter One, "If you're not listening to your company's quarterly earnings call, you don't know what's going on."

Marie Mouchet, vice president and CIO of The Southern Company Operations and Southern Nuclear, advises her employees to read the "boilerplate" information at the end of company news releases. This standard closing paragraph clearly articulates the organization's core business and mission. Marie tells her employees and individuals she is mentoring that this can be a valuable tool in understanding how resources get allocated.

Remember the exercise about allocating resources you did earlier in this chapter? Every enterprise's management—particularly public companies—expends its limited resources where they will generate the best return on investment. This is clearly stated in the company description in the boilerplate news release copy. If you know what this statement says, you'll understand what makes your company's heart beat, and where you and your department fall in the order of priority.

Where can you find copies of your organization's news releases? Check the website again. Look for a section called Press Office, Newsroom, Media, or Investors. You'll be amazed at the information you'll find there!

You might also choose to approach someone fairly senior in the Finance Department. After all, these are the people who track revenues and expenses for your company, so if they don't have answers to your questions, who does? Here Jacqui Welch advises, "Use your Human Resources business partner to help identify and then facilitate an introduction to someone in Finance who would be willing to spend time to help you understand the company's business model."

Of course knowing your organization isn't limited to understanding how it generates income. Just as important is having a good handle on how things get done in your company. And this has multiple implications.

To truly thrive in your job, it's important that your personal operating style matches that of your organization. For instance, if you're someone who enjoys a highly collaborative, consensus-driven workplace, you are much less likely to find professional satisfaction in a company that places a premium on individual achievement.

Conversely, if you chafe at the thought of work teams, brainstorming, and committee assignments, you're more apt to flourish in an environment that recognizes and rewards the individual contributor.

So when developing your own career plan, it just makes sense to invest the time up front to make an honest assessment of your own work-style preferences. Neither of those described above is better than the other, just different. Being clear about how you prefer to work will lead you to ask the right questions and investigate the job environment before accepting a new role.

Finally, understanding how a company operates, internally and externally, means being clear about its values. Most of us would agree that one of the most critical criteria in choosing a life partner is shared values. Should it be any different, or less important, when choosing where we'll spend the majority of our waking hours for years and years?

In practical terms, how are an organization's values reflected? Start with the way it treats its most important resource—its people. Are employee contributions and talents recognized, valued, and appropriately rewarded?

And by rewarded I don't just mean with money. Meaningful rewards are tailored to the individual. For some this may mean earning more paid time off or the opportunity to volunteer in the community during work hours. Others may crave peer recognition through awards and internal communications.

Bottom line, employee rewards are truly meaningful when the individual is recognized as just that—an individual with unique needs and desires. Can you say this is applicable in your workplace? If not, that should give you pause. Is this really the kind of organization you want to work for?

I'll wrap up this chapter with a workplace story that's one of my favorites. For several years I had the great pleasure of reporting directly to one of the most caring, highly intelligent, successful business leaders I've ever known. He was president of our business unit within InterContinental Hotels Group.

I happened to be in his office one day right around the time of his fifth anniversary with the company. He was rifling through the mail on his desk as we talked when he came across a large envelope. His curiosity piqued, he quickly opened it.

Imagine his surprise to find a letter addressed *to* him personally, *from* him personally, thanking himself for his five years of meritorious, dedicated service to the company. The envelope included a "highly coveted" five-year service pin. He was *not* amused.

Clearly the Human Resources department was cranking out standardized letters to all employees, over his signature, with the same content and same reward. What kind of message does that send? Needless to say, this particular recognition policy was changed immediately!

Time for a few more short-and-sweet quiz questions about your organization before moving on to Chapter Three:

Are You a Good Match For Your Organization?

- What is your organization's work culture like? Collaborative? Focused more on the individual contributor?

  _____

- Does the work culture support your preferred work style?

  _____

- What are the "hot" areas for career advancement within your company?

3. For purposes of this book I'm using the term "business model" in a very simplistic way, meaning how the organization generates income.

Don't blame the boss. He has enough problems.
—Donald Rumsfield

Going to the trouble to understand the person you report to and his or her goals and objectives is essential to defining and creating *your* role in the organization over and above your job description. The reality is that you're in a relationship with this individual, and making any relationship work takes effort, patience, and commitment to a shared vision.

Whether you get along well with your supervisor, have a hard time doing so, or feel your relationship is just okay, it's important to remember that, first and foremost, your boss is a human being. He or she deals with the same daily challenges of balancing commitments, coping with stress, family problems, and the full assortment of issues that confront us all. Add to that the responsibilities of leadership, and this person has a pretty full plate.

People in supervisory and leadership roles want to work with those who don't just identify problems but bring solutions to the table. Because your boss *is* first and foremost a human being, he or she doesn't have all the answers. That's where you can bring value.

But how can you formulate solutions if you *a)* don't fully understand how the business works (see Chapter Two), and *b)* don't know what's important to your boss? You can't.

In the classic *Harvard Business Review* article,

"Managing Your Boss," John Kotter and John Gabarro suggest several critical ways to understand your boss, including knowing his or her:

- goal and objectives
- pressures and issues
- strengths, weaknesses, and blind spots
- preferred work style.

What's the best way to go about doing this? It's not as easy as walking into your supervisor's office and using that all-purpose ice-breaker, "Tell me about yourself."

What you can and should do, though, is directly ask your boss to articulate his or her goals and objectives. A logical follow-up would be to ask what is expected of you to help meet those goals and objectives, and to suggest some ways you might do that.

Don't make assumptions that could ultimately derail your relationship with your boss and perhaps even your career. You must be absolutely certain your understanding is crystal clear in this critical area, so there's no better way to get it than directly from the horse's mouth.

Making sure you have a good grasp of the context in which you'll be performing your role and working to meet your boss's expectations is just as important. You need to be aware of any pressures, issues, and challenges related to your supervisor's goals and objectives. What are the criteria for achieving success, the timeline for getting there, and the milestones along the way? Are there resource, legal, or competitive issues you need to know about?

To conduct your reconnaissance here, you can use some of the same tools you employed to learn about your organization's business model. Scour annual reports and listen to quarterly earnings calls to determine what parts of the business may be underperforming and which are growth vehicles.

Maybe your work group is under pressure to improve results. If so, in what way? Is there a demand from higher up for new products and services, or for decreasing costs? Are there political or environmental pressures that must be addressed? Information is power, and you must take responsibility to be informed in order to maximize your value to the organization as well as to your boss.

Once you have a clear understanding of the environment in which you and your boss are operating, you can move on to assess his or her strengths, weaknesses, and blind spots. Your own powers of observation are key here, but you'll want to supplement those with appropriate due diligence. After all, you're playing for big stakes—your career and your personal job satisfaction.

What do I mean by "due diligence"? Again, it consists of doing your homework. Talk to a broad group of people who interact with the boss: co-workers, clients (internal and external), vendors, and others in the community. What do all these individuals say? Listen carefully.

With input from multiple sources in hand—and don't forget to use the Internet to learn about your boss's community engagement, awards and recognition, and so on. Analyze the feedback for themes that could give you insight into strengths, weaknesses, and blind spots.

For instance, if a number of people relate that your boss places a high premium on personal loyalty from those who work for him or her, you might want to look at this more closely. Valuing loyalty above all else could be a sign of insecurity that creates a blind spot in evaluating team members, which could impact you. The chances of actually changing your boss's behavior in this regard are likely very slim, so bear that in mind before undertaking any effort to do so.

While being aware of your supervisor's blind spots is important, it makes sense to focus your energies on discerning the boss's strengths and understanding how you can support those.

If your boss is an excellent speaker, for example, but doesn't actively seek opportunities to speak publicly, you could have a direct conversation with him or her about this and propose some concrete ideas to leverage that ability. For instance, you could point out that participating on industry panels and speaking at community events shines a favorable light not only on the individual but on the organization he or she represents. Such public appearances often surface opportunities for new clients, new partnerships, or other valuable outcomes. When you make those suggestions, also propose some ways you can help make them happen. That adds real value.

We've discussed blind spots and strengths, but what about those troublesome weaknesses? Here's another area where you can bring significant value to both your boss and the organization.

Let's say that you work in a Research and Development group. Your boss is a genius at creating new applications for existing products, often ones that nobody even needs. Or do they? Maybe your boss is a great inventor but somehow totally missed getting that marketing gene. Think about this for a minute. Does anybody really *need* a free iPhone app that makes you feel like you're stapling something? (I'm not making this up—Google it.) This is an extreme example, but you get the picture.

With a more practical example, like satellites, our minds reel. Imagine if the scientists who created the first satellites had limited their vision exclusively to space exploration. Most of us can't conceive of functioning today without our smartphones, GPS, and streaming video on our computers and televisions. All these are satellite-supported products we didn't know we needed fifty years ago—now we can't live without them!

Perhaps you're not the marketing person who is going to identify markets for new product and service applications, but you *can* be the person who identifies the value of including a marketing person in your work team who could perform that role.

Bottom line: information is power, and you are now in a better position to shape your own actions. Let me clear here. I am not suggesting that you exploit the weaknesses of your boss; rather, use that knowledge to create perceivable value for yourself as you work to help your boss succeed.

Now consider your boss's work style and how that affects you. Suppose you keep submitting detailed reports and proposals to your supervisor and never receive any meaningful response. It could be that your boss is a listener, not a reader.

Peter Drucker introduced this concept in his book *The Effective Executive.* If your boss is a "listener," you're much more likely to get the feedback and direction you need if you conduct your briefings in person rather than through written materials.

Conversely, if your supervisor routinely responds to verbal briefings by asking for a written assessment or more research and analysis, you might be reporting to a "reader." This simply means the boss prefers to read and consider information privately before giving further direction or feedback. If that's the case, accept and respect that work style and use it to your advantage. Look at it this way, you're going to get practical writing experience that will serve you well in many areas of your life.

If you are considering accepting a new position within your current company or another organization, how do you find out about your soon-to-be boss's work style? A good starting point is with the Human Resources representative who is placing you in your job. Whether that person is a recruiter or your HR business partner within the company, chances are he or she will know a good bit about how your supervisor interacts with the team.

For instance, you can find out whether your presumptive boss is more of a hands-on manager or someone who likes to delegate, and whether he or she tends to be a listener or a reader. Your HR partner will likely have already directly experienced the boss's work style and can provide you with a heads-up.

Here's another important aspect of work style to consider: Some bosses are better than others at communicating across their group. If your supervisor is someone who clearly articulates the organization's current opportunities and challenges, and who then further articulates the focus and deliverables for your work group, you're fortunate. Many don't.

If you're part of a large group of employees who don't

get clear communication from your boss, then it's your responsibility to yourself and your own success to get the information you need. And you want to be smart about how you do this.

As you think about how to approach your boss, remember that leaders are looking for solutions, not more problems. It's better to approach him or her in a positive way rather than opening with a line like, "You never tell us what's going on. How can I get my work done if I don't understand what's happening?" Come on, would you like to hear that from your relationship partner? Well, your boss doesn't either.

Instead, frame your request for information in a positive way that will signal your boss that you want to help him or her succeed. Your opening line might go something like this, "I'm excited about this project, and I really want our team to look good. What specifically do you need for me to know and do to make this work?"

The implication here is that when the team looks good, the boss looks good. You've not cast any stones regarding the boss's communication skills; in fact, you've just positioned yourself as a team player willing to go the extra mile.

If you already hold a managerial position within your organization, think about your own work and leadership style. Are you empowering your employees with the information they need to make everyone successful?

One of the most common sources of dysfunction I've observed in internal communications are the managers who attend management briefings created to cascade information down through an organization and then just don't do it. The information stops with them. Hard to believe? Think about it. Is this true for you?

I'd like to leave you with one final, important observation relative to understanding and working well with your boss. It is quite simply this: remember who you work for. This probably sounds silly on the surface, but I assure you it is not. In fact, a lot of people make career-ending mistakes because they forget this.

Here's what I mean. You report to your boss, but you work for the organization, and that is where your loyalty should lie. Your contract for employment, whether written or verbal, is with the company, which is the source of your paycheck. Unless your boss *is* the organization by virtue of being the owner, you should be very clear about the difference.

Let me give you a personal example. During the course of my long career, I reported directly to several company or division heads. Some of these high-ranking executives left the organization while I was working for them. This development, in any company, as often as not triggers a review of the rest of the leadership team, which can result in some if not all of the senior executive's direct reports being replaced.

Despite the many changes that took place at the top during my corporate tenure, I managed to thrive with each new boss. I am firmly convinced this was because I was always loyal first to the organization and second to my boss. And they each knew and respected that.

My job was to tell the leader the truth, to offer the benefit of my advice and expertise, and to bring solutions to the table. Sometimes that meant telling the emperor he was wearing no clothes, but even this level of frank feedback can be done with respect and tact. In the end, a true leader will appreciate the candor.

If you do your homework by getting to know your boss and how to most effectively work with him/her and then stay focused on what's best for the organization, you'll have much less personal turmoil and stress on the job. You'll be happier, and this will come back to you tenfold.

Before moving to the next chapter, take this quick quiz to assess your level of understanding of the person you work for.

How Well Do You Know Your Boss?

What are his or her

Goals and objectives:

_____

Pressures and issues:

_____

Strengths, weaknesses, and blind spots:

_____

Preferred work style characteristics:

_____

※　※　※

CHAPTER FOUR

APPRECIATE THE ROLE OF HUMAN RESOURCES
...as a partner in mapping your career path.

The soft stuff is always harder than the hard stuff.
—Roger Enrico
-

For most of us, Human Resources (HR) is the portal into the organization(s) where we'll spend the majority of our working hours. In this department we have our initial screening and interviews; this is the group that actually issues the formal job offer.

It's HR that administers payroll, ensuring we get paid the right amount and on time. This team implements performance management programs, and they help resolve personnel issues. Last but not least, HR is the door through which we'll exit the organization.

Since HR plays such a significant role in our professional lives, it makes sense to understand its broader role and how that can be leveraged to your advantage.

Many employees don't fully comprehend the complexities of today's HR function, especially in organizations with workers in multiple countries, each with a unique set of labor laws. Human Resources must manage issues and responsibilities ranging from union contracts and worker compensation to negotiating benefit options that are meaningful for the workforce and cost-effective for the organization. Layer onto this the challenges of immigrant worker documentation and the ongoing education required to keep up with changes in regulations regarding pension and retirement plans, among a host of other tasks and accountabilities, and you begin to get a sense of the many facets of HR's contributions to any organization.

Why is it important that YOU understand all this? Remember that knowledge is power, and you want to have the wherewithal to create your own career destiny. If you have a basic understanding of what HR does, you'll be able to work more effectively with your HR business partner to help you help yourself.

As part of my research for this book I spoke at length with two top HR professionals, each of whom have held senior leadership positions with global enterprises: Jacqui Welch, whom you met in Chapter One, and Lynne Zappone, chief talent officer for Popeyes® Louisiana Kitchen. Both Jacqui and Lynne have extensive experience working for companies with thousands of employees in locations across the globe.

I wanted to know how these two leaders would define the role of HR, and how, from their perspective, most employees perceive the function of HR in the organization. Is there a shared view, or a disconnect?

Lynne believes there is indeed often a gap between employees and HR professionals with regard to understanding the role of Human Resources. She notes that when she hears an employee say something to the effect of, "HR just looks out for the company," she quickly and unabashedly agrees. She then goes on to explain to the employee that looking out for the company helps all stakeholders, including employees. When the company is doing well, the employees, shareholders, and customers benefit.

Both Lynne and Jacqui stressed that the HR function is critical to the business. While understanding laws and regulations to ensure organizational compliance is a primary responsibility, it's also crucial that HR understand the problems of the organization and offer solutions that move the business forward.

According to Jacqui, "There is a little bit of schizophrenia about the HR role—both within and outside the HR organization." Technological advances, she explains, have vastly reduced the transactional time required of HR professionals, freeing them up for strategic thinking and planning. That means today's HR leaders should be viewed as integral partners in formulating and delivering on the strategy of the organization.

What does this mean for you? That it's important to get to know your HR business partner, for one thing. Jacqui suggests taking that person to coffee or lunch and asking directly how the two of you should interact.

Your HR person has specific knowledge of the company's strategic direction and will know which groups within the organization offer the best opportunities for career advancement. He or she will also most likely be familiar with the varying work styles within individual departments.

Be sure to ask for insights about your boss—after first asking your HR business partner if it's ok to request this information. Remember, knowing your boss is critical to your success.

As you become more knowledgeable about the company, your HR business partner can support you in planning your career path. While doing your homework to identify the key markers along your journey, keep in mind a useful observation from Lynne Zappone.

Lynne points out that in recent years the career "ladder" has become more of a career "lattice." She attributes this to the flattening of organizations as they have become leaner in order to stay viable. Nowadays there often isn't a clearly defined career ladder, such as the one typified by the traditional brand marketing pyramid. That ladder looks like this:

Today's savvy employees move incrementally, even laterally, across the organization in order to acquire the skills and experience necessary to get where they want to go. By making your goals and ambitions known to HR, you have a much better chance of learning about opportunities that match your criteria for career advancement, remembering that advancement doesn't always mean "up."

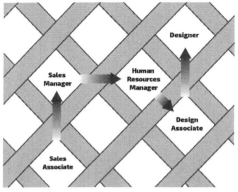

Marie Mouchet's career is a great example of this kind of "latticing" (career laddering). When I met Marie, I was impressed by the fact that she is chief information officer of Southern Company Operations and Southern Nuclear. In my book, serving as CIO for a nuclear power company is pretty much akin to being a rocket scientist. Imagine my surprise when Marie told me that this is her first IT job! *Say what?* It's true. Marie has worked a lattice approach for career advancement that has taken her into the senior ranks of one of the largest utility companies in North America.

After earning a degree in mathematics, Marie began her career teaching math to high school and junior college students. Later at Southern Company, she designed rates and handled rate cases, worked in Regulatory Affairs, and spent years in sales and marketing, establishing the company's first national accounts program.

Marie says that a traditional career ladder wouldn't have worked for her because many of the jobs she held weren't even in existence when she joined the organization. Bottom line—she was smart and aggressively sought out opportunities to gain new skills and experience that would increase her value to the company.

Thinking about Marie's career trajectory strongly reinforces the concept of latticing. Moving from teaching math to marketing is flexing the muscles on both sides of the brain, the left/analytical side as well as the creative right side. This is a great example of someone who refused to be typecast by her educational credentials or early career experience.

Marie and Jacqui Welch each took charge of their own career destinies and made "the system" work for them. Both emphasize the need to think strategically about your aspirations, to utilize all the resources available to you—including HR—to further your ambitions, and finally, to be observant and opportunistic.

None of us can afford to wait for opportunities to fall into our laps. Opportunity is like happiness—we make our own. Understanding and internalizing that fact propels us into action. Don't make the mistake of thinking that HR is responsible for recognizing your value and contributions to the organization and making sure you're meeting your career objectives. That's your job.

Jacqui Welch adds that a good HR professional will always challenge any employee who inquires about moving into a new position. The HR person will (or should) ask questions such as, "Why do you think you are well-suited for this particular job? Tell me more about your understanding of the job and how your skills line up with that role. Who are you grooming to take your current position?" Jacqui believes it's important that employees accept responsibility for developing the people who will come behind them.

From my conversations with Jacqui and Lynne I've distilled the following list of erroneous assumptions that are almost certain to derail, or at a minimum stall, anyone's career. Be on the lookout for these "potholes" and avoid stepping into them at all costs!

Top 10 Assumptions That Can Keep You From Getting Ahead

You assume:
- People understand how valuable you are to the organization even if you don't tell them.
- Management will recognize and reward you even if you don't let them know, on a regular basis, what you've accomplished.
- You will get promoted just because you are talented and work hard.
- If you are assertive, people won't like you.
- It's important that everyone like you in order to advance.
- Keeping up with workplace politics is a no-no. (I don't mean "getting involved" with workplace politics is a no-no. This is typically not a good idea. However, being aware of the politics in the workplace is just being smart. Knowing which way the winds are blowing will help you stay afloat.)
- Networking means connecting with people you like and know.
- The salary or raise you are offered is the best final offer.
- If you negotiate for a raise it will be viewed negatively.
- Opportunities will surface solely because of your excellent track record.

It's up to you to ensure your contributions are noted. It's your responsibility to create your career strategy and your job and to be listening when opportunity knocks. Use HR to help you help yourself.

As we close this chapter, take a minute to make some notes:

Partnering With HR For Career Success

Who is your HR contact?_____

Have you ever initiated a one-on-one discussion with your HR partner to apprise him or her of your career goals? What are some points you would like to make in such a meeting, and questions you would like to ask?_____

Are you open to "latticing?" (career laddering) If so, do you have a plan or vision of how that might work for you?_____

❋　❋　❋

CHAPTER FIVE

FIND YOUR MENTORS
...and learn to value diversity of thought.

"In learning you will teach, and in teaching you will learn."
—Phil Collins

What's all the buzz and fuss about mentors? We're constantly hearing business consultants and coaches go on about how mentors can be critical to an individual's success. But how? Why?

The answer is really pretty simple. If life and career are analogous to a journey, it's a cinch the trip will be easier with a map, GPS, or guide.

When traveling to a new city or country, isn't it great to know someone who's been there and can give us insider tips on hidden-gem restaurants, advice for getting around the area, and a list of locals' favorite spots for shopping, relaxing, and hanging out? It's also quite helpful to have a friend in the know tell us what to avoid—such as the over-priced restaurants and shops that cater strictly to tourists.

Taking this analogy even further, it would be terrific to have a network of "inside guides" in *all* the new cities and countries we visit. In fact, this is such a good idea that businesses that do just that are flourishing in today's connected world. Think Yelp, TripAdvisor, and others that may pop to your mind.

So in life as well as career, it follows that we'd want more than one mentor to help guide us through the many new areas we encounter along the way. Really, wouldn't it be cool to have mentors like Yelp contributors who could tell you, "That company looks great from the outside, but if you work there you'll find out it is all sizzle and no substance."

Without even realizing it, we've all had mentors at one time or another. Our parents and teachers are mentors, and friends can be as well. In our careers, first bosses are often mentors, and I count myself extremely lucky to have had some good role models early on in my career.

A good career mentor can coach you in developing specific skills and areas of expertise. But this same mentor may not be the best person to help you understand the organizational waters, pointing out dangerous currents, hidden rocks, and turbulence.

A friend and former colleague of mine, Kirk Kinsell, is president of the Americas region for InterContinental Hotels Group (IHG). When I asked Kirk about business mentors who had influenced him, he quickly named three individuals who had had a profound effect on his life, both professionally and personally.

According to Kirk, one of his earliest mentors was the legendary Trammel Crow, the enormously successful Dallas-based Real Estate developer. Crow keenly understood the value of relationships—to the extent that he pioneered the concept of including key associates as equity partners in his deals. He demonstrated for Kirk the fundamental principal that people will stick with you through both good and lean times if they have a vested interest in the business.

Another valuable lesson Kirk says he learned from Crow is that if you truly love what you're doing, then work is play. For Trammel Crow, the two were indistinguishable.

I don't think I've ever viewed play as work. But I can honestly say that at many points in my career, work was so much fun it did seem like play. There were times when I said to myself, "I can't believe I get paid to do this!"

Another important mentor for Kirk was Dan Weadock, former president and CEO of Sheraton Hotels. At the time of their working relationship, Sheraton was part of the conglomerate ITT, a very numbers-driven organization.

Weadock was also numbers-driven, and not particularly relationship-driven. To work well with him, Kirk discovered, one had to understand the importance of performance metrics and the equal importance of having a solid plan to keep improving those metrics.

Kirk's third mentor is Mike Leven, currently president and chief operating officer of Las Vegas Sands Corp. Kirk's first meeting with Leven took place in the early 1990s when Leven was appointed president of Holiday Inn Worldwide, the predecessor to IHG. Kirk received a call from his current boss, the company's CEO, informing him that Leven had been appointed to the newly created position of company president, and that he, Kirk, would be reporting to him. The CEO directed Kirk to be in Leven's office first thing Monday morning.

Kirk explained to the CEO that he couldn't meet with Leven on Monday because he had a firm family commitment that day and wouldn't be in the office. Though somewhat flustered by Kirk's position, the CEO acquiesced.

Upon meeting Mike Leven the following Tuesday, Kirk apologized for not being there the day before to greet him and explained his prior family commitment. Leven stuck out his hand and said, "I'm going to enjoy working with you. You've got your priorities straight."

The most valuable lesson Kirk says he learned from Mike Leven is the importance of values-driven leadership. Leven demonstrated through his own commitment that family and community come first, with work supporting those important priorities.

Three very different mentors, with three distinctly different approaches to business, each profoundly affected an individual's life and career and how that person now mentors many others.

Kirk's experience has taught him that in a formal mentoring relationship, it's important for both parties to manage expectations from the very beginning. The mentee should be clear on what he or she needs. Both parties should agree on a mutually acceptable way of working. For instance, will there be regular face-to-face meetings, or will phone calls and e-mails be the primary form of communication? Just make sure everybody is singing from the same song sheet.

Often senior executives like Kirk are not involved in structured mentoring relationships with many of the people they mentor; these leaders simply live their values and model behaviors in a way that others want to emulate.

Take a minute to contemplate that. When we think of mentors, we usually focus on people who positively impact our lives. In fact, the vast majority of business leaders are honorable women and men who sincerely want to, and do, conduct business in an ethical way.

But in recent years we have seen so many business scandals play out on the world stage—outrageous misdoings that have brought down governments, caused entire economies to collapse, and irreparably disrupted, and sometimes destroyed, the lives of millions of people. For many of us, the financial misconduct that led to the Great Recession of 2008–2009 still impacts our finances and psyches. Before that there was the savings and loan crisis of the 1980s and 1990s, followed by the collapse of the junk bond market in 1990 and the transgressions that came to light about Enron in 2001, WorldCom and Tyco in 2002, and HealthSouth in 2004. The list seems to go on and on.

I inject this cautionary note to illustrate the importance of defining our individual, personal values and following our own moral compass. If we know where the lines are that we will not cross under any circumstances, we are at far less risk of committing behaviors and actions we will later regret.

Most of us benefit from having a whole team of informal mentors. The composition of that team can, and in all likelihood should, change from time to time as we develop and grow. It's also important to seek out mentors who have different backgrounds and perspectives, who can provide diversity of thought that will better inform our views and perspectives. In other words, we need mentors who will stretch us.

We should also give a nod to the importance of reverse mentoring, which, like traditional senior/junior mentoring, provides valuable perspective for both parties. I'll give you a somewhat humiliating personal example (and please don't laugh).

Several years ago when texting was becoming a major communications tool, I was totally perplexed by the whole phenomenon. As a busy executive addicted to my BlackBerry, I couldn't understand why someone would bother to send a text when e-mailing was just as fast. Or what the heck—do something old fashioned like pick up the phone and call the person.

One day I mentioned this to a much younger colleague (Amanda, you know who you are). She responded by informing me that, *a)* not everyone had a BlackBerry with e-mail/data capabilities, Ms. Executive Person, and *b)* texting is so much faster and easier than actually calling, or even e-mailing. She went on to explain that when you call someone on the phone you spend time on meaningless chatter like, "What's up? How ya doin'?" then listening to a response that may not truly interest you. Whereas with a text, you can be succinct and to the point without the time-consuming banter.

Immediately I understood the appeal of texting. Now I'm a total "textaholic" (is that a good thing?) and find it so much easier to connect with people that way. *Everybody*, it seems, responds to texts.

This is a very simplistic example of reverse mentoring: an older, seasoned executive learning from a much younger colleague. Understanding the rationale behind something as simple as a technological innovation that was inconceivable in my youth has truly changed my life...I think for the better.

Would you say the following statement is true or false? "In society today there is widespread awareness and acceptance of the value of diversity and inclusion in business."

It's probably safe to say your answer to this question is largely driven by your own experiences. We know our view of the world is shaped by gender, age, ethnicity, religious beliefs, sexual orientation, and more, so doesn't it make sense that we could each learn and benefit from the perspectives formed by *others'* experiences?

Imagine this: You're on your first trip abroad, to Hong Kong (or any city—you pick the place). As you settle into your hotel room, you turn on the television and search for CNN International because you know it will be in English. After watching this program on several occasions during your stay, you are astonished at the world view presented outside your familiar surroundings. The news is not dominated by the politics of your native country; in fact, the media coverage regarding your country puts events in a different context than you've ever considered. It makes you think . . .

Here's another interesting scenario: This time you are traveling by train from Amsterdam to Paris, a trip that takes a little more than four hours. It occurs to you that this is about the same amount of time as train travel from Boston to New York. By comparison, though, the Amsterdam/Paris journey speeds you through three entirely different countries en route, each with a different language, government, set of customs, and so on.

There's no question that Boston and New York are very different from each other and offer residents and visitors alike a unique experience. Having said that, the two metropolitan areas are united by language (more or less), a federal government, shared history, and more.

For me, actually experiencing the proximity of countries in Europe for the first time shone a whole new light on the two world wars of the twentieth century. It helped me comprehend the longstanding grudges and distrust among citizens of certain countries. Through this experience I was also able to better understand the various views of my own country that many people in Europe hold, and sometimes these views made me quite uncomfortable.

Has something similar ever happened to you? Has hearing a different viewpoint on a topic that previously was crystal clear in your mind caused you to pause and reconsider? Hopefully you *are* someone who has experienced this, because it is an unmistakable characteristic of a person seeking to be a continuous learner and striving to grow through knowledge.

Often in the workplace we encounter situations that occur as challenging because one or more individuals seem to hold views that "come out of left field" and certainly don't align with our own. What's our initial reaction—to dismiss the person as clueless? Or maybe we get angry because we feel he or she "ought to know better."

The views and attitudes we hold as adults are shaped by our childhood environments and formative years. Most of us know and accept that, but sometimes it's hard to even imagine backgrounds dissimilar from our own, especially conditions and circumstances of which we have no personal knowledge.

In today's world, people are generally aware of differences based on the obvious—race, gender, and ethnicity. But interestingly, one of the biggest challenges facing today's workforce is the issue of conflict within multi-generational work teams.

Why has this become so common? One obvious answer is that people are living and working longer. It's not uncommon today to know people in their seventies or eighties who are still working, either out of economic necessity or love of what they do.

Thinking about the different perspectives shaped by race, gender, ethnicity, age, and other factors, doesn't it make sense to seek mentors who reflect at least some of these various perspectives? After all, how can we learn, grow, and influence others if we don't have the advantage of a world view broader than that driven only by our own personal experiences?

Much has been written and discussed throughout the past few decades about diversity as it pertains to race and gender. We won't re-till that ground here; rather, I invite you to focus specifically on the issue of diversity of thought and work style within multi-generational teams.

Let's start with some readily available data measuring generational attitudes regarding workers of other generations. Some of these findings may shock you, so be prepared.

First, some definitions. The term "Baby Boomers" we are all pretty familiar with, referring to individuals born in the post-World War II baby boom that occurred between 1946 and 1964. The generation that followed, known as Generation X, includes those born in the early 1960s to early 1980s. Generation Y, or the Millennial Generation, consists of individuals with birth years from the early 1980s to the early 2000s.

In a recent study conducted by the research firm Millennial Branding on behalf of financial giant American Express [4], data showed that while many employers value Gen Y workers for their perceived expertise with technology and social media, 47 percent of those surveyed said Millennials have a poor work ethic, 46 percent said they're easily distracted, and 51 percent said they have unrealistic compensation expectations. *Whoa!*

This same study found that Gen Y workers, by contrast, had a much more positive view of their managers, believing their supervisors can offer experience (59 percent), wisdom (41 percent), and a willingness to mentor (33 percent).

Another interesting finding was that 73 percent of managers are very willing or extremely willing to support Gen Y employees who want to advance within the organization, but fewer than half of the GenYs surveyed (48 percent) are either very interested or extremely interested in making such a move. *Latticing, anyone?*

If the attitudes described above don't make you a little uneasy, how about the workplace tensions that arise because of positions held about the ever-popular "work/life balance?" It's not uncommon for childless Gen Y workers, as well as empty-nest Baby Boomers, to feel more than a little put out when employees with children at home seem to be given more flex-time consideration because of parental demands.

What about the Boomer who is caring for aging parents? What about the Millennial who wants to learn a second language, or pursue some other endeavor that is a high priority in his or her work/life equation? Looking at this objectively, it's easy to see that one person's priority doesn't translate as a priority for everyone else.

According to an article by Hannah Seligson in the *New York Times*, "Work/life balance, which sounds so wholesome and reasonable, can be a zero-sum game in the office."

Seligson further notes that one person's work/life balance can be another's work/life overload. As a result, many Americans who work for companies that embrace flexible hours are confronting a type of office class warfare.

How do you defuse tensions that arise because of these kinds of issues? Seligson quotes advice from Cali Williams Yost, chief executive of Flex and Strategy Group/Work and Life Fit, a research and consulting firm: "Remove the why—take the reason out of it" when asking for time off or a more flexible schedule.

Williams Yost continues, "You shouldn't say, 'I'm leaving at 3:00 p.m. to take my kid to a soccer game' because what about the person who has to take a parent to chemotherapy or the person who needs to go to a marriage counselor?"

Just thinking about all these potential emotional powder kegs makes my head hurt—yours, too, I'll bet. I'm sure you're getting my point, so let's move on to explore the process for identifying mentors to help you navigate these tough waters and how to secure their help.

In the previous chapter we looked at the ways Human Resources can help you design your career path, and in many organizations HR offers a structured mentorship, or leadership development program. Unfortunately, though, in many companies these programs are available only to certain levels of employees, often excluding large groups of individuals who could benefit tremendously.

If that's the case in your organization, take heart. This book is all about taking charge of your own destiny, so I'm going to suggest ways to find your own mentors and structure a relationship that works and provides benefit for you both.

Finding a mentor isn't complicated—just look for someone who has what you want. It's important to stress here that having defined success for yourself is a prerequisite to being able to zero in on mentors who will bring you the most value.

For instance, let's say your exercise in self-discovery has revealed that, for you, success is tied to landing an executive leadership role in a major corporation with significant monetary rewards. You believe the key to achieving this is determining, early on in your career, the moves along a career ladder or lattice that will advance you steadily toward your goal.

Given this, it would seem intuitive for you to look for successful leaders who have worked their way up through the organizational ranks to seek their advice. You'll want to ask about such topics as recognizing and capitalizing on opportunities and building teams. Identifying individuals in leadership roles who share a similar background with you—educationally, socio-economically—to serve as mentors might also seem to make sense.

However, while it may seem logical to assume all leaders work their way up through the various organizations where they work during the course of their careers, this is absolutely not always the case. Think about those who have been recruited and achieved their positions because of celebrity, family ties, or social standing.

These people can be valuable mentors as well because they bring different perspectives to problems and challenges. Though it might not be realistic to attempt emulating their path to leadership, understanding their viewpoints and experiences can be invaluable as you are called on to lead more and more diverse groups.

Finding mentors who share your values and have

achieved success as you define it is indeed important, but equally critical is including mentors on your team who are the opposite of you. After all, the primary function of your mentor is to challenge you and help you expand your horizons, grow, and learn. What better way to get out of your comfort zone than by seeking advice and direction from someone who operates very differently than you do?

Now that you've identified one or more desirable mentors, how do you approach these individuals and convince them to say yes to mentoring you? Many people I've talked with throughout the years say this is the hard part. It doesn't have to be!

Let's use another analogy here—dating. When we meet someone we'd like to get to know better and perhaps even have a relationship with, our initial approach isn't to ask for a big commitment. We ask the person to have coffee or lunch, or maybe to see a movie. (On second thought, with the price of a movie and popcorn these days, that's a pretty big commitment.)

So, we meet for coffee or lunch. Sometimes that highly desirable person turns out to be fabulous, and other times not so much. The same thing happens with potential mentors.

Knowing this, wouldn't it be better to start out asking potential mentor candidates if you could buy them coffee or lunch to get their advice or pick their brain on a *specific* topic? In taking this approach you accomplish the following:

By identifying up front a specific question or issue you'd like to discuss, you demonstrate that there is a purpose for your request for the individual's time.

By asking only for a short time commitment (coffee or lunch), you are being respectful of this busy person's time.

You haven't made any commitment that you may later regret. You didn't immediately ask this person to be your mentor only to find out you have zero rapport or chemistry. Just as in dating, don't rush into anything!

You haven't triggered a flight instinct in a super-busy person who might think you're looking for a bigger commitment than he or she is prepared to make. Again, as with dating, your prospect may want to keep things casual.

After you've secured that all-important first "date," you and the potential mentor will probably know instinctively whether you want to continue the relationship. If you do, you'll need to establish some ground rules right away, such as whether you will create some regular structure for your relationship or reach out on an as-needed basis.

We've focused so far on the traditional view of mentoring—that of a junior worker seeking out a senior executive for advice and counsel. While this is by far and away the most common type of mentoring, I want to circle back around to the concept of "reverse mentoring," which I touched on earlier. Savvy executives understand the value of this mirror image of the conventional model. Let me give you an example.

I recently had the opportunity to hear Marie Mouchet give a talk about the importance of mentoring. During her presentation, Marie mentioned the value she'd received through reverse mentoring. I subsequently interviewed her to get a more in-depth explanation of her views on the subject.

What Marie said really clicked. In a nutshell, reverse mentoring balances out the mentor/mentee value equation. While the mentee gains from learning about the mentor's life and career experiences, the mentor benefits from the fresh perspectives and insights into new ways of doing things. Value for everybody!

One of the examples that Marie used—and one that truly resonated with me—was about a mentor who asked her mentee to provide tutoring on a new social media program. Specifically, Marie asked a younger, "techie" person to set up an internal "Yammer" account for her. This Yammer account allows managers within Marie's organization to send short messages to their work teams—much like Twitter, but customized.

The value for Marie was that she got a hands-on, personalized tutorial on a new technology. It also demonstrated to her employee/mentee that she wants to continue to learn.

For the mentee this provided an opportunity to engage with a senior leader on a personal level, a chance to be recognized for particular skills and expertise, and an opening of lines of communication—a win/win.

Sometimes perceptions across multi-generational work groups can create issues. Here's an example that again involves technology.

Gen X'ers and Millennials grew up using technology that wasn't around when Boomers were coming of age and entering the workforce. These younger workers are much more accustomed to multi-tasking on computers and cell phones while also engaged in another activity.

It's common these days to see younger employees bring laptops and cell phones into meetings and proceed to type and text away during a presentation or discussion. Older workers may view this as distracting or even disrespectful and make judgments about the individual based on that perception. These judgments can be career killers.

There are a couple of easy ways to diffuse this particular situation. First and foremost the event leader should communicate in opening remarks what electronic devices are permissible for use during the meeting. If this does not happen, the employee desiring to use electronic devices should check for approval to use the device(s) and state why the devices will be used.

As an aside on this topic, it will probably be fine with the meeting leader/presenter if your stated purpose is to make notes of the meeting. It will probably *not* be fine to hear that you plan to work on another project while the meeting is in progress. A gray area would be recording a presentation, especially if the presentation is given by a paid speaker. There may actually be a clause in the speaker's contract that prohibits unauthorized recording.

While this is a very specific example, it illustrates a key point, and the bottom line is this: if you are unsure how your actions will be perceived, ask in advance. This is the kind of thing you could easily discuss with a mentor.

Another benefit of multi-generational mentoring relationships is the opportunity to have candid discussions about issues that shape perceptions on both sides of the age divide. Here's an example from my personal experience.

At one time I had an extraordinary young woman on my team who was bright, articulate, hard working, and extremely productive. She was "the package." So what was the issue? Quite simply, she dressed as though she were still in college.

While we did have a business casual dress code at my company at the time, leadership (at least one or two generations older than the employee described here) definitely dressed in a manner that was much more business-like than truly casual. This young woman's appearance conveyed a subtle message that somehow she hadn't made the transition from the classroom to the office.

Unfortunately for this young woman, she was perceived by most of the leadership team as someone who was a highly competent project manager but not someone with the executive presence to make the next professional leap. Eventually she became frustrated and left the company. To this day I wish I had been more direct in my feedback to her so that she would perhaps still be with the company.

The lesson here goes back to Chapter Two and "knowing your organization." This includes being attuned to its culture. If you work where innovation, creativity, and individualism are the order of the day, then what you wear to work probably isn't a big deal. On the other hand, if you work in a conservative environment, you're well-served to pay attention to how the influencers dress and conduct themselves.

If this example has made you uncomfortable and perhaps made you think, "Nobody is going to tell me what to wear," then I strongly recommend you go back to Chapter One and review your personal definition of success. What kind and how many concessions are you willing to make to achieve your success?

These are important questions that should be answered after much thought and consideration. Knowing who you are and what is important to you is the first essential ingredient for thriving in the workplace. A good mentor can counsel you wisely in personal areas like this on subjects you may not feel comfortable discussing with your boss.

As with any relationship, there will be expectations on both sides of the mentoring equation. From the mentee perspective, clearly there is an expectation of advice and counsel. But the mentor has expectations, too.

According to Kirk Kinsell, in order to determine the ROI on time invested, the mentor will look for what action the mentee takes based on the advice and counsel offered. Kirk notes that the mentee always has the right to reject any advice offered, but if that is the case, the mentee should explain to the mentor why the advice was rejected. The implication here is that if there is no expressed reason for *not* acting on advice, the mentor expects to see some action.

As this chapter closes, I hope I have convinced you of the value of mentoring, both for the mentee and the mentor, and given you a comfort level for approaching potential mentors. After all, it isn't a lifetime commitment...

You know the drill by now. Before moving onto the next chapter, think about and answer the questions below.

-

Making Mentoring Work for You

Do you have a mentor or team of mentors?

_____

If so, what is the focus of each member of your team of mentors?

_____

Has your team changed over time? How?

_____

If you don't currently have a mentor or team of mentors, what areas of your life could benefit from finding a mentor to advise you?

_____

What is your plan to find the mentor(s) you need?

_____

4. "Gen Y Workplace Expectations" released by Millennial Branding and American Express in September, 2013.

❋　❋　❋

CHAPTER SIX

IDENTIFY YOUR "ADDED VALUE"
...then create your own opportunity.

One's real worth is never a quantifiable thing.
—Malcolm Forbes

According to *Investopedia*, "Individuals can bring added value to services they perform, such as bringing advanced financial modeling skills to a position in which the hiring manager may not have foreseen the need for such skills."

Another example would be finding that brilliant neurosurgeon who also has charisma, a fantastic bedside manner, and the ability to easily convey complex medical jargon in terms the patient and family can understand. Calling Dr. Sanjay Gupta?

In today's employment climate, it's not just about pulling your weight. Employees must earn their keep and illustrate why they are exceptional at what they do.

Don't take for granted that your boss and superiors know everything you are doing, including the successes you've notched on the job. Unless you aren't getting your work done, many bosses leave you alone and rarely check in.

It's up to you to keep your boss informed on a regular basis regarding what you are accomplishing. Think about your supervisor's preferred style of receiving information (remember Chapter 3?), then devise a plan to keep him or her informed. If your boss likes to read and digest information before discussions, then by all means write a brief monthly report to outline the goals you've met and the solutions you provided that meet the strategic plan of your company or department. Be as specific as possible, including metrics where applicable, because you are building your own personal brand.

If your boss is a listener and prefers to receive information through verbal updates, then get time on the calendar on a regular basis to bring him or her up to speed. Don't book a lot of time, and certainly position your updates as a benefit to keep your supervisor adequately informed about progress toward strategic priorities.

These mini-reports will provide facts to validate your contributions to the organization. And importantly, you will gain valuable face time with your boss in a proactive rather than reactive way. Plus, the process of developing your reports will help you keep track of what you have accomplished, so you can talk about this effectively during your performance evaluation and beyond.

Every encounter with your boss in which you don't come bringing a problem or asking for something (more money, more staff, a time extension on the project) increases your worth. Trust me on this one: supervisors never feel satisfied with employees who always put another burden on their shoulders!

You want your boss to be glad to see you and to view you as a problem-solver. This is another characteristic of your personal brand that will always stand you in good stead.

Become a go-to expert in your area, providing solutions for problems and anticipating issues before they arise. Position yourself as someone the company can't afford to lose, and your chances for advancement will increase dramatically.

Additionally, think about what else you bring to your job that creates added value and puts you ahead of your peers. Are you the person who's always asked to train new team members on job specifics that go beyond technical skills training? If you are, there probably is a good reason. Most likely you are an effective communicator, have good interpersonal skills, and are a true team player. How can you leverage these abilities so they are viewed as a value-add at performance review time?

Perhaps you're the person who always volunteers to lead the departmental update at staff meetings. Are your presentation skills strong enough to position you for appearances (and therefore career visibility) in front of upper-level senior management, perhaps even the CEO and Board of Directors? If so, I assure you this is true added value.

Maybe you're the designated hitter when the boss needs support and documentation for his or her presentation to senior management. Are your data always reliable? Do you deliver in a timely manner? If this ability falls outside the scope of your regular responsibilities, it raises your personal capital considerably.

You may determine that you need to develop additional skills or gain new knowledge to advance or assume expanded responsibilities. Consider this an investment in your career and ask for opportunities to acquire the skills and knowledge you need. Doing so demonstrates that you want to grow and are willing to take on new challenges in order to do that.

Do you remember the concept of latticing that was discussed in Chapter Four? Sometimes the smartest thing you can do is to move laterally within an organization in order to get the experience you require for that next big role. People who choose to make a lateral move are often surprised to discover it has put them in a sweet spot they never would have envisioned embarking upon along the career highway.

Being indispensable will also help make you *less* vulnerable when mergers, layoffs, and right-sizing occur. I stress the word "less" here as, sadly, nobody is immune to layoffs these days. All the more reason you should take every opportunity to learn, stand forward, and grow your network of relationships, both inside and outside your company.

Despite the dismal job market of recent years, there *are* opportunities. For instance, a study conducted by the firm Millennial Branding and the online career network beyond.com revealed that 30 percent of companies surveyed lost 15 percent of their Millennial employees in the previous year. The reason most often stated for leaving: not a good cultural fit. But hey, one person's cultural dissonance with an organization might be the very reason it would be a great fit for someone else. So there is opportunity in that 15 percent!

Don't think, though, that keeping your head down at work and focusing on doing the best you can day in and day out is going to bring opportunity knocking. You'll need a plan for seeking out opportunity and pursuing it.

Remember Lynne Zappone from Chapter Four? Lynne has a great story about how she not only sought out opportunity but chased it across country.

She was twenty-three years old and about to graduate with a bachelor's degree in Education from Flagler College in St. Augustine, Florida. Through her experience as a student teacher, Lynne had learned she loved to teach and she had the ability to inspire.

But after a couple of years, she realized the career opportunities offered by teaching didn't really interest her. She wanted something more.

As fate would have it, just before she had to sign her contract to teach the following year, Lynne attended an in-service training session focused on a new health curriculum that would include interactive skills and experiences. She was so impressed with the woman who facilitated the discussion that she had the proverbial a-ha! moment.

Lynne said to herself, "I want *that* job. I want to lead adults through discussions. I don't want to teach for thirty years."

So what did she do? The only sensible thing she could do, of course. She moved from Florida to California with no job in sight.

Once she arrived on the West Coast, she immediately started looking for a job in Training And Development. She got lots of rejections but kept applying for positions while supporting herself with sales jobs, working at temp agencies, and even managing microfiche (look it up) at a library.

She also worked for an entrepreneur in a job conducting product interviews all day. At this point in the story, Lynne stresses the importance of recognizing and appreciating any crazy, unexpected thing that falls into your lap and helps propel you toward your goal. In this particular job she learned how to do behavioral interviews, a critical skill for the kind of HR work she was seeking.

Through her network of friends and colleagues she found out about a training job at the Sheraton Universal Hotel in Los Angeles. She *wanted* that job!

Lynne started doing her due diligence to prepare for the interview. She researched the company, learned as much as she could about a new guest service training program Sheraton was launching, and studied career guidebooks.

She had a successful initial interview. The hotel HR director wanted her to meet the entire team. Then she had to meet the regional head of HR for Los Angeles. So far, so good.

The final hurdle was an interview with the corporate Director of Human Resources for Sheraton at company headquarters in Boston. Lynne says the man was lovely in her first interview with him, despite the fact that he purportedly wanted someone with an academic degree in training or a related field.

She went through six separate interviews that day, ending back with the Director of HR. Lynne said to herself, "I want this job, and he's gonna stop me from getting it."

So with nothing to lose, Lynne said to him, "I get the impression you have concerns. Please tell me what they are so that I may address them."

His head popped up—he was stunned she was that confident and that forward. For each area he brought up, she had a ready answer. He later told Lynne that if she hadn't boldly asked him about his concerns, he wouldn't have offered her the job.

Without that very first "real" job in her chosen field, Lynne says she wouldn't have had the job and career she has today. She created her own opportunity.

After two great years with Sheraton, the training position was eliminated and she was out of work. So she took a job at a bank, in the Organizational Development–Financial Services department.

The financial services industry shares similar characteristics with the hotel business—money management, technology, and direct customer contact. Her skills were transferrable, and this new job gave her more opportunities to design and develop programs. She learned and grew.

Fast forward to the present. Lynne is Chief Talent and HR Officer at Popeye's Louisiana Kitchen. Along the way to this position she worked in three distinct industries—lodging, financial services, and quick-service restaurants. Throughout her career, Lynne has asked herself, "What are my core skills that transfer across industries?" and continued to create opportunities for herself.

She points out the importance of helping the hiring person see how your skills transfer. Corporate recruiters, Lynne notes, have a natural bias against employees without industry-specific experience.

Let's think about that for a minute. The ability to sell ideas, to persuade others to your point of view—this is something intangible that makes one employee stand out from the others. I'd say that is real added value, wouldn't you?

You may have the coolest new product in the company's history or an idea for a new revenue stream or perhaps be perfect for a new role in the organization, but if you can't effectively sell your vision, it's not likely you'll get the necessary backing to move forward. So, if you have the ability to influence others, you have a marketable skill—a skill that can transfer across industries. The question is then, how do you leverage that added value?

Think back to Chapter Four where we looked at the role of HR. Have you done everything you can to ensure your HR contact knows not only how well you perform the requirements of your job, but also what you consider your core skills and the additional value you bring to your role? You want that person to become an internal advocate for you so that when an opportunity does open up within the organization, whether advancement or a good, strategic lateral move, your name is top-of-mind.

Let's focus now on identifying your added value. Defining added value is as simple as determining what you contribute beyond the skills and expertise required to do your job that are set forth in your position description. How do you help the organization succeed?

Sometimes it's hard to identify your own added value. If you find that to be true for yourself, it's a good idea to turn to your friends and mentors to help figure this out. Here's a simple exercise you can use to get the ball rolling.

List below ten adjectives or nouns you would use to describe yourself:

_____

_____

_____

_____

_____

_____

Now ask your mentor(s) and a few co-workers to make similar lists.

_____

Most likely you'll see several characteristics repeated between the two lists. Use these words to define your added value. Are you intuitive? Structured? Creative? Empathetic? Flexible? Driven? Perfectionist? Storyteller?

Look carefully at the words used to describe you. Now think about how those words translate into behaviors. If "flexible" is a word that applies to you, then you probably tolerate change well. This may mean you are well-suited for fast-paced, ever-changing work environments. Chances are good that it also means you are comfortable working with a certain amount of ambiguity. This would be big added value in a job with a start-up organization or one that is undergoing significant change.

If you are a perfectionist, then you will add real value in any role requiring meticulous attention to detail. This includes many positions in design, manufacturing, research, and finance, to name just a few.

When I asked Kirk Kinsell about his appointment as president of the Americas region for IHG, I asked specifically about his added value. What was that special something that made him stand out in a field of highly qualified competitors for the job?

Kirk says the added value he brings is his ability to be human and recognize other aspects of employees' lives beyond the workplace. He views his core purpose as helping others, and he works to help people understand how they can be successful in *life,* not just business. Makes a lot of sense, if you think about it.

When people are successful in their personal relationships, when they live harmoniously within their communities, and when they generally feel good about themselves, it stands to reason they would be happier at work. A business leader with the desire and ability to help employees succeed in all aspects of their lives is a true leader. That leader definitely adds value to the organization by engendering loyalty among employees and contributing to a happier, healthier, more productive workplace. This is the kind of environment where employees thrive.

Kirk also points out that you must keep working on yourself in order to help others. I'll use the analogy of the airline safety briefing that instructs, "Put on your own oxygen mask first before attempting to help others." It's a pretty critical instruction, isn't it? After all, how can we help someone else when we're struggling for breath ourselves?

I'll close this chapter, as with all the preceding ones, with a short quiz. As you continue on your journey of self-discovery, focus on identifying those personal attributes you can leverage, and you'll find your added value. Once you recognize how you can bring additional value to your job, think about how those same attributes can be employed to enrich your relationships and your life in general. You and all those you touch will be the better for it.

Starting with the ten most-repeated words used to describe you by your mentor(s)/friends/co-workers as well as yourself in the exercise earlier in this chapter, define a set of behaviors that accurately describe your added value.

Word/Behavior

Example: Intuitive - Good at reading customer body language.

1. _____
2. _____
3. _____
4. _____
5. _____
6. _____
7. _____
8. _____
9. _____
10. _____

※ ※ ※

CHAPTER SEVEN

BUILD YOUR LEGACY
...and don't wait to get started.

If your actions create a legacy that inspires others to dream more, learn more, do more, and become more, then, you are an excellent leader.
—Dolly Parton

As you've reached the last chapter in this book, I hope you have taken the time to truly reflect on the tips and guidance provided in the preceding chapters. If you did this, you should have a deeper understanding of your own definition of success and how you can shape your experience of the workplace.

Now it's time to take a moment and look further into the future, to what meaning and purpose you want your work life and career to have—to consider your legacy.

As we think about the concept of legacy, it's easier to envision our own if you know what is important to you and what you stand for. Remember that simple quiz you took in Chapter One? (You *did* take the quiz, right?) Go back and revisit your answers, as they are the clues to what your legacy will look like.

Like your definition of success, your idea of a legacy will likely be very different from that of many of your friends and peers. That's the way it should be, since we are all unique.

I love Dolly Parton's quote that opens this chapter. It asserts that our legacies aren't something we strive to create at end of life to have "something to leave behind."

Indeed, our legacies are all about what we're doing today, how we're living our lives now. Our legacies are how we help others spiritually, intellectually, physically, and financially, and how we facilitate positive relationships with and among others. To leave a legacy is to live a life that serves as an example of what an exceptional life can look like.

While Dolly Parton leaves a powerful legacy as a truly authentic songwriter, singer, and entertainer, her legacy is much more than that.

In 1986 Parton became a co-owner of Silver Dollar City in Pigeon Forge, Tennessee. The theme park was subsequently renamed "Dollywood." In 2010, Parton said, "I always thought that if I made it big or got successful at what I had started out to do, that I wanted to come back to my part of the country and do something that would bring a lot of jobs to this area."

Dollywood now employs three thousand people, making it the largest employer in that community.

Several years ago I attended a conference on philanthropy, and one of the speakers took the participants through an exercise that stays with me to this day. Let's try it together now.

Close your eyes and visualize the skyline of any major city in the United States. Now mentally remove all the public buildings and spaces that were built through personal philanthropy. I'll use the city of Chicago since it is a city I know and love.

In Chicago we'd take away the Field Museum, Shedd Aquarium, Millennium Park, the Joseph Regenstein Library at the University of Chicago, and Wrigley Field, to name a few. These extraordinary places contribute significantly to the quality of life, not only for Chicago residents but also for the millions of people from around the world who visit them and benefit from web access to collections and events.

Take another example, in another place. Performing at Carnegie Hall in New York City is the dream of millions of musicians around the world. To say you've played Carnegie Hall means you've reached the pinnacle of artistic success. I believe Andrew Carnegie would have loved that. Carnegie would also have loved the fact that millions of people have had access to books and learning opportunities at the nearly three thousand public libraries bearing his name around the world. He would have been equally proud of the eighteen Nobel Laureates from Carnegie-Mellon University.

While many, many people know the Field Museum, Shedd Aquarium, Wrigley Field, Carnegie Hall, and the other landmarks I've mentioned, how many people know about the business contributions of Marshall Field, John G. Shedd, William Wrigley, Jr., or Andrew Carnegie? All these men were giants of business and industry, from retailing to steel manufacturing. Their business achievements were extraordinary, but their passion for serving and helping others was equally so. Wealth and vision enabled each of these individuals to leave legacies that have survived for generations and will live on well into the future.

Great wealth certainly provides a platform for creating a lasting legacy. Wealth creates family fortunes that can be handed down through generations, providing opportunity for philanthropy across decades—even centuries. For many of us, though, that isn't likely to happen.

A study called "Inheritance and Wealth Transfer to Baby Boomers" 5 published December 2010. Commissioned by MetLife from Boston College's Center for Retirement Research, says that two out of three Boomers in the United States should get a monetary inheritance, with $64,000 being the median amount. The study anticipates an intergenerational transfer of wealth totaling $11.6 trillion, including some $2.4 trillion that has already been gifted.

This huge transfer of wealth, perhaps the largest mankind has ever seen, has been and is being handed to Boomers by their parents, famously known as the "Greatest Generation." Economists of future generations are going to have a great time examining the long-term results of this monumental monetary shift!

Having grown up during the Great Depression, Boomers' parents are famously frugal. The Boomers themselves—not so much. Couple the Boomers' traditional spending and saving (or lack of saving) patterns with the vagaries of the markets these days, and who knows how that great transfer of wealth will play out over time.

Will the Boomers be good stewards, leaving some of their parents' financial legacy to their children? In more positive financial times it might turn out that way, but with today's struggling economy and the extraordinarily high unemployment rates for Boomers it's also quite likely that this won't be the case.

While I'm certainly not a financial advisor, my opinion is that if you're a member of the Gen X, Gen Y, or Millennial age groups, it would be wise to start thinking about a Plan B. Assume the worst case scenario and don't count on a legacy of wealth from your parents.

Perhaps you've heard people say they inherited their parents' work ethic. This is a powerful and lasting legacy. Indeed, a person with a strong work ethic has the ability to make more than one fortune, and that's a great Plan B for wealth and/or financial security. So if I truly believe our legacies are all about what we're doing and how we're living our lives today, why do I start this chapter by talking about financial legacies? To underscore the point that wealth is fleeting.

Don't get me wrong—I've got nothing against wealth. Quite the opposite, in fact, financial security has always been a cornerstone of my personal definition of success. However, it is not the *only* thing that defines my success, neither, I would guess, yours either.

So aside from wealth, what makes a powerful legacy? It only takes a minute of focused consideration to conjure up a list of individuals who, despite their lack of financial resources, have made a lasting impact on the world:

- Martin Luther King, Jr.—advocacy for non-violent change
- Mother Theresa—compassion and a life of tireless service
- Anne Frank—inspiring millions through her diary
- Walt Disney—imagination and determination
- Nelson Mandela—social rights leader and first post-apartheid president of South Africa
- Neil Armstrong—space exploration
- Helen Keller—champion of people with disabilities

Surely you could add many, many names to this list. One thing is for sure, though—no matter how long the list, and diverse their legacies, all those individuals would share one common characteristic: they lived their lives to the fullest and pursued their interests with unlimited passion.

Each of the individuals I listed above also used non-cash assets to create their legacies. Wittingly or unwittingly, they gave their talents and that greatest gift of all—time—to make a lasting mark on this world.

What do I mean by non-cash assets? These are the characteristics that make us who we are, and they are the very things that contribute to personal legacies, whether good or bad. Make no mistake about it, many people do leave bad legacies. Adolf Hitler and Idi Amin are two names that jump immediately to mind.

Let's pause here to take a personal inventory of non-cash assets. Check all that apply to you from the list below:

___ Performance talent (e.g., music, acting, art, speaking, sports)

___ Name recognition

___ Business skills/acumen (finance, marketing, technology)

___ Social skills (networking, relationships, contacts)

___ Willingness to serve and volunteer

___ Items that can be used to help others, (perhaps items that could be used to raise funds?)

___ Others (list them here)

_____

Take a moment to come up with a few examples of how such non-cash assets have been used to make a difference.

In the field of entertainment alone there are many. The singer Bono is someone who has raised millions of dollars for philanthropic causes through benefit concerts and recordings. He has even been nominated for the Nobel Peace Prize! With his immense wealth, it's quite likely he makes personal donations as well, but he has no doubt raised considerably more through use of his talent.

Willie Nelson, a founder of Farm Aid, staged countless benefit performances to raise money to save small family farms. He energized his huge fan base to support family farmers.

During his lifetime, comedian Danny Thomas raised millions of dollars to fund St. Jude Children's Research Hospital in Memphis, Tennessee. Today that hospital is known around the world for the care provided and research conducted to save the lives of children from every segment of society.

Danny's daughter Marlo Thomas builds on her father's legacy by continuing his fundraising efforts, and the hospital grows and prospers.

"America: A Tribute to Heroes" was a benefit concert created by the heads of the four major American broadcast networks: FOX, NBC, ABC, and CBS in the aftermath of the September 11 attacks on the World Trade Center and the Pentagon in 2001. Actor George Clooney organized celebrities to perform and to man the telephone bank.

Top names from the music industry, including Bruce Springsteen, U2, Celine Dion, Goo Goo Dolls, and many more donated their time and talent to raise money for the families of victims of the attacks and families of the first responders who died during rescue and recovery. More than $200 million was raised.

Another great example is the late Princess Diana, who used her fame and name recognition to accomplish immense good. In particular, she brought awareness to the issue of land mines that continue to kill and maim people years after the end of conflict. Her legacy of charitable work, including the focus on land mines, is being carried on by her sons, Princes William and Harry.

Fame and name recognition can be a bit tricky, though, especially if the individual suffers a very public fall from grace. Lance Armstrong presents a cautionary tale here. His LIVESTRONG™ Foundation raised hundreds of millions of dollars for cancer research. Later, his admission of drug use caused him to be stripped of his Tour de France cycling titles and put his foundation on the rocks as donations plummeted in the wake of the scandal.

For those of us (myself included, in a big way) who don't have abilities in the realms of art, entertainment, and sports, it can be difficult to determine exactly what talent we possess that could be leveraged to benefit others. Let me just say here that I have yet to work with a nonprofit that wouldn't be thrilled to attract supporters and board members with strong technology, financial, and marketing skills!

In the area of business expertise and acumen, there are people volunteering and donating their time and talents every day to help others start and grow their own businesses.

SCORE, the Service Corps Of Retired Executives, is a wonderful example. The volunteers at SCORE are successful businesspeople from across industry segments who have retired but are willing, even eager, to share their skills, expertise, and years of practical business experience to help others succeed. SCORE volunteers counsel and provide direction on all aspects of business, from creating a business plan and constructing realistic sales volume and expense forecasts to marketing, technology, and more. These volunteer executives are true mentors.

I want to spend some time here focusing on social media skills. There's so much talk these days about social media—networking through LinkedIn, Facebook, Twitter, Pinterest, and other online sites, blogging, and on and on. All these communication and networking channels potentially have value when used effectively.

It's fun and challenging to rack up five-hundred-plus connections on LinkedIn and scores of endorsements for personal skills and expertise. Likewise, it's a kick to add new "friends" on Facebook and followers on Twitter and a personal blog. Take a moment, though, and make a candid assessment of all these connections. Are they contacts, or do you have a relationship with each individual?

The point is an important one; there is a big difference between contacts and relationships. Contacts are names in your personal database and can easily be people you've never met. Perhaps you have made a connection through a business associate or mutual friend. While contacts can be helpful in many instances, they should not be confused with relationships.

Relationships, whether good or bad, have context. They are based on shared experiences and often on shared interests. The best relationships are treasured and nurtured over time. This means staying in touch, albeit infrequently perhaps, during good times as well as bad times. Relationships are built on having a sincere interest in the other person.

When we take the time to cultivate good relationships with others, surprisingly positive, serendipitous things can happen. I want to share an example with you here.

A little more than four years ago, a young man I'd come to know through my volunteer work with a well-known and respected humanitarian organization contacted me, asking for a meeting. This individual, Derreck Kayongo, is an African-American in the literal sense—he was born in Uganda and subsequently immigrated to the United States. Prior to coming to the United States, he had been a refugee in Kenya during the years of Idi Amin's dictatorship in his home country. I had heard a little of his personal story but was about to learn something that would change my life forever.

Knowing I'd spent my professional life in the hotel business, Derreck asked me what happened to the little bars of used soap left in guest rooms after the guests check out. I told him that the bars are thrown out and ultimately end up in landfills around the world.

His next question stunned me. "What if," he asked, "we could collect that discarded soap and make it into new soap to be given away in refugee camps?"

Derreck went on to explain that the leading cause of death for children under five years old living in refugee camps throughout the developing world is upper-respiratory diseases and diarrhea caused by poor sanitation and improper hygiene. A big part of the sanitation and hygiene problem is lack of access to clean water and *soap*.

Instantly I knew this was a problem the hotel industry could do something about. I also knew hoteliers would want to do this because it was such a simple, no-brainer idea. Donate something that's going into the trash anyway, help save a life. Who wouldn't want to do that? And, oh yes, by keeping all that soap out of landfills, we also help keep the chemicals in the soap from leaching into the groundwater as it decomposes.

While it wasn't likely that hoteliers alone could solve the clean water issue, they could help make soap available to those most vulnerable people who, either can't access it or can't afford it. Get ready to rumble!

Shortly after Derreck reached out to me, I contacted the president of the Georgia Hotel and Lodging Association and asked him to hear the idea. He agreed it had merit and arranged for Derreck to speak to a group of hoteliers, as a way to test the concept.

When Derreck made his presentation, he signed up thirteen hotels on the spot to participate and donate discarded soap. Thirteen hotel operators saw the opportunity to make a positive difference and leaped at it.

We were on our way, and the Global Soap Project (GSP) was born.

Through personal relationships with a diverse group of professionals, Derreck and I put together our very first board of directors. Each individual invited to serve this little start-up nonprofit was targeted because of specific skills and expertise we knew we were going to need.

The GSP founding board comprised an attorney specializing in international law, a communications and PR professional, a web and social media guru, a hotelier, a nonprofit professional, a broadcast media specialist, and a Gen Y business professional.

The organization was launched with no start-up capital. We had no assets other than the used soap Derreck picked up from the hotels, transported in his personal vehicle, and stored in his basement. But we had friends. Good friends.

Every board member used personal relationships to help us obtain donations of everything from warehouse space to a basic website to the cost of shipping the very first container of soap that traveled from the United States to Africa. Volunteers worked to turn the used soap into new.

Board members also chipped in funding for legal filings, our first piece of soap processing equipment, utility bills, and other costs. We scraped along like this for two years, often scrambling to cover an unexpected expense.

Then, through a long-time friend I'd worked with years before, the GSP team was introduced to the executive at Hilton Worldwide in charge of the company's sustainability initiatives. Several months later, after appropriate due diligence and discussion, Hilton Worldwide became the first corporate partner of GSP, providing $1.3 million in funding, to be disbursed over the course of three years.

Today GSP is growing and thriving. Distribution partners include the Centers for Disease Control, CARE, the United Nations High Commission for Refugees, and many others. We are shipping soap around the world, currently to more than thirty countries. And we are helping to save lives.

In Malawi alone, we have been able to document sharp reductions in the number of early childhood deaths attributable to lack of sanitation and proper hygiene. Importantly, we are teaching people the critical, life-saving power of soap. Ideally, the people who are currently receiving free soap will someday be financially capable of purchasing soap from local sources and will *want* to because they understand the true value of soap.

In 2011 Derreck Kayongo was recognized as a CNN Hero. In fact, he was one of the ten finalists whose stories were shared before a television audience of millions in December 2011. The recognition was a resounding validation of Derreck's idea and will forever be a part of his legacy.

This is a much abbreviated story, but one that I hope demonstrates the power of relationships. With zero cash assets, a group of passionate, dedicated people were able to tap into personal relationships and create something powerful that is changing and saving lives around the world.

If what Derreck accomplished seems like something outside your reach, look around you for other examples. Perhaps you've been fortunate enough to become friends with people who give of themselves to serve others and make life a little easier for those in need. Some of these friends might volunteer through their place of worship, while others may take a secular approach by donating their time through organizations such as their city's "Hands On Network," local food banks, homeless shelters, centers for domestic violence, PTA, support agencies for people with disabilities, and so on.

Every community has an abundance of nonprofit and charitable organizations in need of volunteers to help fulfill their mission. These valuable volunteers are building their personal legacies, and their good works make an impact that often is felt far beyond the people directly served.

Service to others is a powerful legacy, and the rewards are tremendous. I think often of my long-time neighbors, Greg and Lynn Stiles, who do so much good work through their church and neighborhood school PTA and by helping local families in need. Following their parents' example, their sons Nicholas and Corey started as pre-teens participating in mission trips to Appalachia. The boys raised their own money for the trips and performed manual labor as part of their responsibilities on the missions (something their parents would jokingly say isn't too common at home). Serving others is ingrained in these young men. Service is part of their DNA, and a great legacy of their parents'.

Michael Thurmond is another great example. As of this writing, Michael serves as the Superintendent of Schools for Dekalb County, Georgia. The district serves nearly one hundred thousand students and employs more than thirteen thousand. He was sought out for this position during a time when the school district was sinking into insolvency and facing a possible loss of accreditation, as well as being very visibly involved with the criminal prosecution of a former superintendent.

What in the world would move Michael to leave a lucrative career in the private sector, after having already served three highly lauded terms as Commissioner of Labor for the State of Georgia? Before that he had served as head of Georgia's Department of Family and Children's Services. Earlier in his career, he had become the first African-American from Clarke County since Reconstruction to be elected to Georgia's General Assembly.

A little personal history on Michael will give you some insight into his character. He was born in rural Georgia during the time of the Jim Crow laws that well pre-dated the Civil Rights Movement in the United States. He is the son of sharecroppers and the first member of his family to graduate from college.

Not only did he graduate from college, he graduated cum laude with a BA degrees in both Philosophy and Religion from Paine College and later earned his juris doctorate from the University of South Carolina School of Law. He also completed the Political Executives program at the John F. Kennedy School of Government at Harvard University.

Michael Thurmond could have written his own ticket—and indeed he did. For Michael, service to others was of paramount importance, and he used his education, tenacity, and personal charisma to build a career and life legacy based on service.

Working with the most vulnerable and impressionable populations—families and children in crisis, people struggling to find work, people with disabilities, and children in need of a quality education—Michael has worked tirelessly to innovate, build coalitions, persuade, reach across political party lines, and do whatever was necessary (so long as it was ethical and legal) to better the lives of thousands, if not millions, of people.

Here's an example of how Michael has worked quietly through the years to get the job done. During his term as Georgia Commissioner of Labor, the Department of Vocational Rehabilitation was part of the Labor Department. Michael saw that people with disabilities generally comprise an under-valued, under-served segment of society. At the time, Georgia had a significant number of citizens with disabilities and, sadly, as the wars in Iraq and Afghanistan raged, those numbers were increasing steadily.

Georgia military personnel were returning from war with traumatic brain injuries, post-traumatic stress disorder, missing limbs, and impaired vision and hearing. Working through the staff at the Roosevelt Warm Springs Institute for Rehabilitation, located relatively close to the huge Army base at Fort Benning, Georgia, the Department of Labor reached out to the Warrior Transition Command. Could the two entities work together to serve these service personnel and their families as they moved out of the Army and into the new realities of their lives as people with disabilities?

They could indeed. Michael Thurmond, Georgia Commissioner of Labor and a life-long Democrat, reached across the political aisle to collaborate with the Governor of Georgia, a Republican, to convince the State legislature to earmark $10 million for construction of a new residential and learning facility, designed especially for people with disabilities, at Roosevelt Warm Springs Institute for Rehabilitation. That $10 million in State funding was matched with federal dollars, enabling the construction of a state-of-the-art facility befitting, among others, the brave men and women who sacrificed so much for our country.

I'm sure Michael never consciously intended to create this facility to build a legacy for himself. But it *is* part of his legacy, just as much as his leadership in rescuing a school system in crisis, helping people build skills that will land them jobs, and so much more. This is who he is. He serves.

Perhaps you're thinking, "Yeah, right. I'm never going to be elected to public office. I won't have those kinds of opportunities to make a difference."

But there are countless other examples around the world. Maybe you will identify with Jonny Imerman, a cancer survivor who started Imerman Angels, a nonprofit that pairs cancer patients with cancer survivors for one-on-one support. Since 2002, Imerman Angels has made eight thousand matches worldwide.

Maybe Catalina Escobar's story will resonate with you. Catalina founded a group that provides support to teen moms in Colombia, where one in five girls ages fifteen to nineteen is or has been pregnant.

Then there is Thulani Madondo. He started a program to provide academic support to four hundred children who live in the slums of Kliptown, South Africa. Madondo is a lifelong Kliptown resident, and he has a goal of helping people change their lives and their community through education.

If none of these examples seem within your capabilities, then just check out the CNN Heroes website. It's full of stories about ordinary people doing extraordinary things. Most of these heroes operate their programs on a shoestring, counting on the support of other ordinary people like themselves. They are living their legacy.

Think about a time you had the opportunity to help someone. How did it make you feel? Pretty good, right? For most of us, helping others is energizing, giving us the chance to feel part of something bigger than ourselves. It adds another layer, or dimension, to our world and makes it seem significantly brighter.

By now I hope you are thinking seriously about the legacy you are creating. This last chapter was designed to stimulate ideas regarding your own non-cash assets and how you might use them to build your legacy. Take a few minutes now to revisit that list you worked on earlier in this chapter. For good measure, here are a few additional examples of non-cash assets to help get your creative juices flowing.

- Land (community garden, teaching garden)
- Second language (volunteer translator)
- Vacation home (time period donations for charity auction)
- Your additional ideas:

_____

_____

_____

_____

_____

Now comes the hard, but exciting, part. How can you leverage these assets to build your legacy? What are you going to *do*?

Creating a legacy isn't like a school or work project. It doesn't require a strategy paper with lots of supporting tactics, action timelines, and so on. What it requires is your willingness to pursue the dreams and visions that are meaningful to you and that will help people spiritually, intellectually, financially, or in terms of their relationships with others.

It is never too soon, or too late, to start acting on our dreams. Go ahead. Nothing is stopping you!

5. *"Inheritance and Wealth Transfer to Baby Boomers," Commissioned by MetLife from Boston College's Center for Retirement Research, published December 2010.*

※　※　※

Twenty years from now, you will be more disappointed by the things that you didn't do than by the ones you did do. So throw off the bow lines. Sail away from the safe harbor. Catch the trade winds in your sails. Explore. Dream. Discover.

—Mark Twain

Now you know what you need to do. The question is, are you going to do it?

Your first reaction is likely to be, "Of course I'm going to do it! If I didn't want to be happy and thrive at work, I wouldn't have read your book."

Really?

How many times have each of us had good intentions, determined to take charge of our lives and make some positive changes? Then the crazy stuff starts happening—and that crazy stuff, my friend, is called life!

We all have to deal with the unexpected things that life puts in our path, day-by-day and almost minute-by-minute. The secret to happiness and contentment is how we deal with these unexpected things.

It's all about the mind-set. Do you approach challenging situations with a view that you can positively influence the outcome? Or do you resign yourself to feeling powerless in circumstances that "happen" to you?

If your take on life, including your professional life, as that of a passive participant, you relinquish the huge opportunity to fashion yourself into the person you yearn to be. Think of it this way: if you were driving down the interstate and saw a car swerving into your lane, wouldn't you take action to avoid a crash? Of course you would. You're not going to assume there is nothing you can do and just let a crash impact your life, if you can help it.

Okay, so you're committed to taking charge, right? You are going to do whatever it takes to thrive in the workplace. And if you're thriving at work, it will undoubtedly spill over into every other aspect of your life.

Now I'm going to share a little secret with you. Actually, it is not a secret at all. You already know what I'm about to tell you.

If you follow all seven tips detailed in this book, your attitude and approach to work will change for the better—and your boss will notice it. Your co-workers, friends, and family will begin to seek you out for advice. You'll become a mentor, either formal or informal. You'll be sought after for plum work assignments.

People will enjoy working with and being around you and will think of you as a role model. When management and co-workers—present and future—along with the other people in your life think and speak of you, it will be with respect, admiration, and perhaps even affection.

Not a bad legacy.